Intermediate Guide to Free -Motion Quilting

- Few scraps of appliqué fabrics

- 27" fusible web

- 1 1/4 yard backing

- Coordinating threads (to join appliqué shapes)

- 44" by 44" batting

- Safety pins

- 4 1/2"Accuquilt square

- Fabric cutting machine

- Sowing machine

Instructions

Follow these simple steps to design a green pasture baby quilt.

Step 1. Cut 8 two-and-half inches strips; 6 four-and-half inches squares; 5 two-and-half inches squares; 12 two inches square triangles; and 4 sheep bodies backing from the white fabric. Cut the light-blue fabric to 34 1/2" × 18 1/2" rectangle.

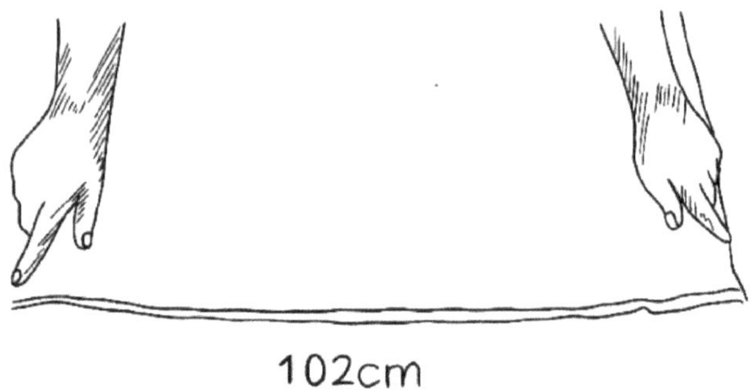

Cut 1 thirty-four-and-half inches by two-and-half inches rectangle; 10 two-and-half inches square; and 12 two inches half square triangles from the green fabric. Cut 8 sheep legs; 4 pairs of sheep ears and heads; 2 sheep bodies; 2 sheep reverse bodies; 6 sun rays' sheep ears; and 1 two-and-half circle for sun.

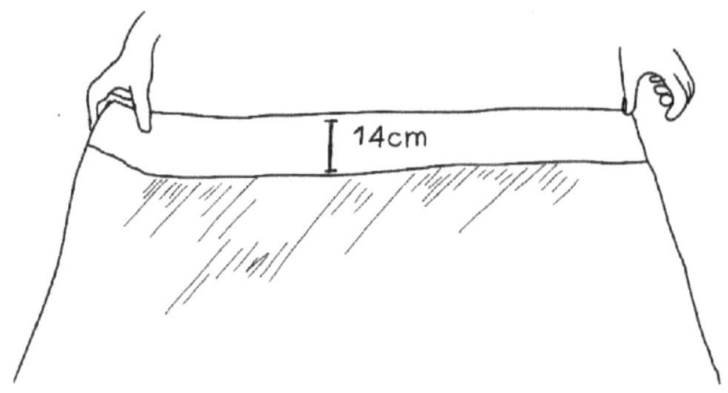

Step 2. Pin 5 sets of white and green fabric, as well as the two-and-half green squares, and sew them. Pin and sew the white half-square triangles and the 12 green fabric layers. Pin the white half-square triangles and green in pairs and sew them.

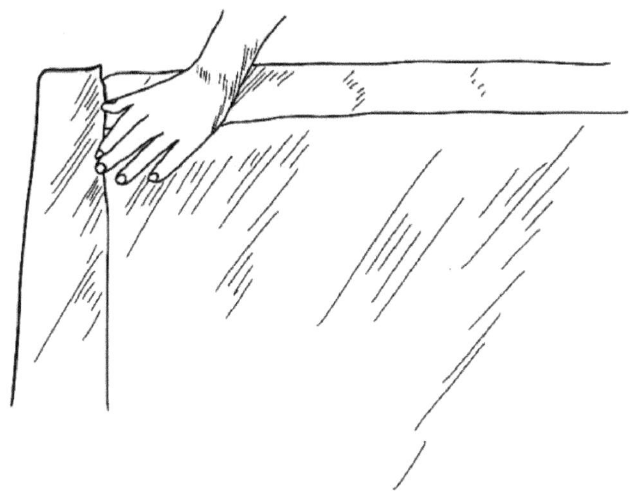

Step 3. Do border fence layout and join the units to finish the border. Join the green rectangle with the light-blue rectangle on a long edge. Pin the fence border to the base of the green rectangle, and get paper backings off the appliqué shapes.

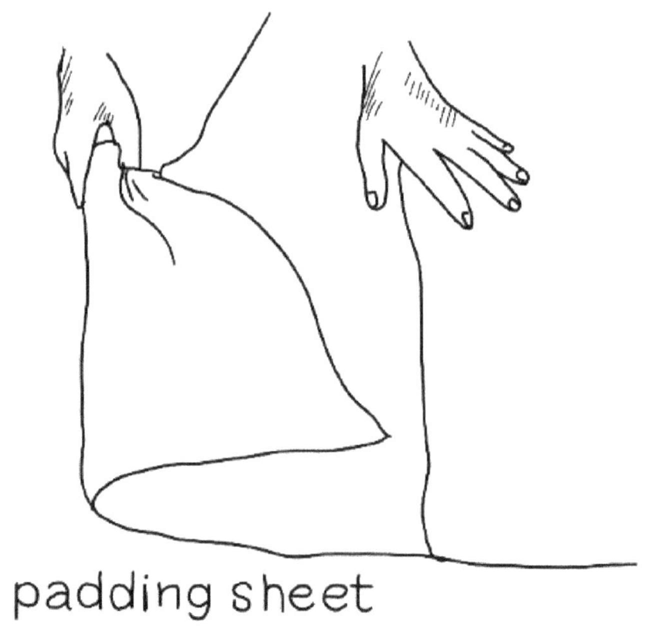

Step 4. Carefully structure clouds, sun, sheep, and sun rays. Fuse in line with manufacturer's instructions.

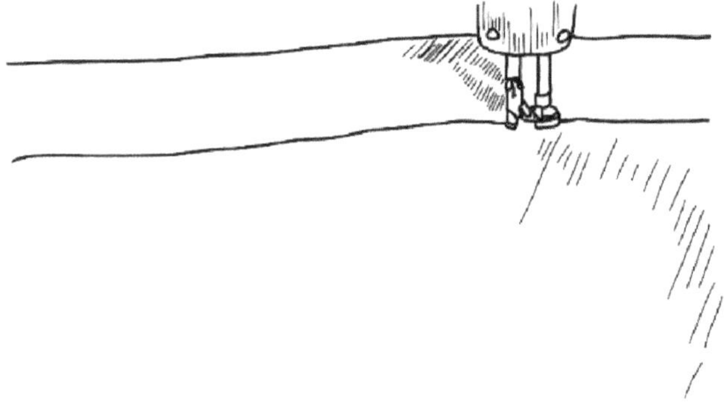

Step 5. Use a machine to appliqué design the edges but only with matching threads such as narrow

satin stitch, matching thread, or narrow zigzag. Add two-and-half white borders to the sides, top, and bottom of the design.

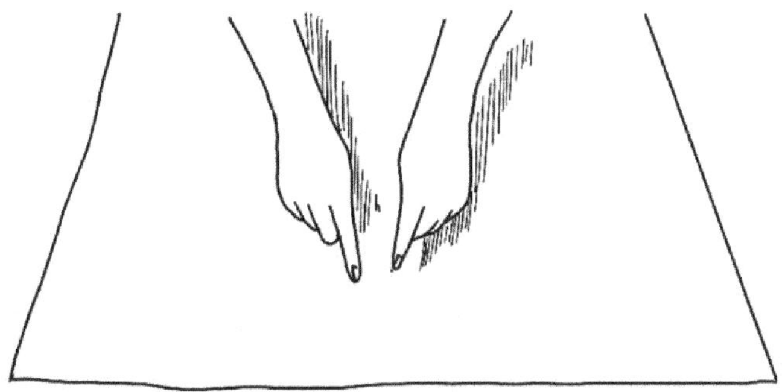

Step 6. Baste backing with quilt top, machine quilt the design, and add binding.

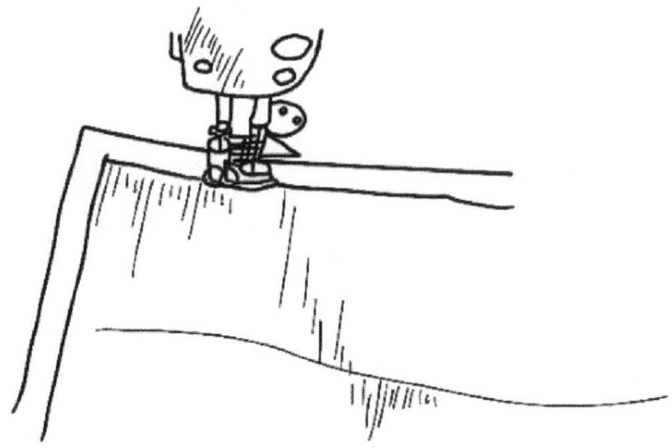

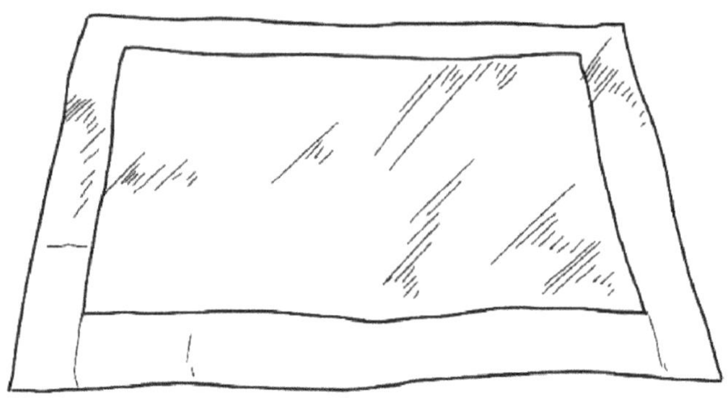

How to Make a Rainbow Baby Quilt Pattern

Call it the end of all baby quilts and you may be right. Just like the radiant colors of the rainbow, this baby quilt pattern is beautiful and appealing to the eyes. It is one pattern you don't get tired of designing. With a bit of creativity, some scraps, or small cuts of fabric, you can design the quilt at the comfort of your home. Here's how to design the pattern.

Required Materials

- Rainbow-colored fabric

- Contrasting-colored fabric (white with red is perfect)

- 36" yard backing fabric

- 1 yard batting

- Fabric for binding (preferably white)

- A pair of scissors

- Thread

- Sewing machine

Instructions

Follow these simple steps to design your rainbow baby quilt pattern.

Step 1. Cut all layers of fabric to 6 1/2" × 28× 1/2" strips.

Step 2. Pick the white square and lay it side-down close to the right edge of your colored strip.

Step 3. Thread and needle your machine.

Step 4. Make a straight line from one corner edge to the other and sew accordingly but make sure you sew on the line.

Step 5. Join the white strip but make sure the entire stripes is not more than 30 inches.

Step 6. Repeat the process until you finish sewing the colored strips and attach them to look like a rainbow.

Step 7. Add the batting and trim excess fabric or thread.

Step 8. Do the binding with a 2" white strip.

How to Make a Charm Pack Baby Quilt Pattern

If you are looking for a simple, bright, colorful, and charming baby quilt pattern, end your search straight away. This unisex baby quilt balances tropical colors with novelty prints and its sewing process is super fast. Not only is this charming quilt a perfect gift item for every child, it is very simple to design. With a few tips, you can design a charm pack baby quilt pattern at the comfort of your home. No worries. Here is how to design it.

Required Materials

- Twenty 5" square colored fabric (preferably Club Havana)

- Twenty 5" square white fabric (Riley white is good)

- Forty 5" square white fabric

- 12" binding fabric

- 48" backing fabric

- A sewing machine

- Baby-sized quilt batting

- A pair of scissors

Instructions

Follow these simple steps to design your charm pack baby quilt pattern.

Step 1. Cut the colored fabric to 5" squares and white fabric to 5" × 36 strips.

Step 2. Needle and thread the sewing machine.

Step 3. Lay each white square on a colored square and sew 1/4" from the right side downward.

Step 4. Join a colored square to the remaining side of the white square and sew 1/4" from right downward.

Step 5. Place white strips on colored ones and sew from the bottom edge, leaving out 1/4" seam. Repeat the process until you sewn 8 rows to design the quilt top.

Step 6. Pin your quilt batting and backing in the middle of the quilt top to make a sandwich.

Step 7. Use a diamond pattern to draw diagonal lines 3 inches apart from the top of the quilt downward.

Step 8. Trim excess fabric or thread and add the quilt binding.

How to Create a Patchwork Baby Quilt

The patchwork baby quilt is an appealing and adorable design for the kid you love. Its well-laid pattern and colorful designs make it the go-to baby quilt, and words alone cannot express its uniqueness. Still, this quit is easy to design and you can create it right there in your home. Just a few tips stand between you and this baby quilt. No worries. Here is all you need to create the patchwork baby quilt.

Required Materials

- 42" by 42" batting

- 81 packaged 5" by 5" squares

- 45" fabric for backing

- Safety pins

- 12" fabric for binding

- Sewing machine

Instructions

Follow these simple steps to create your own patchwork baby quilt

Step 1. Spread out the packaged squares. Let 9 stay down while 9 lie across. Also, arrange the colors properly to print an appealing pattern. But, should the color or fabric placement raise concerns, use color to divide squares to two parts.

Step 2. Assign 1 to 9 numbers to the rows and stack the 5" by 5" squares carefully into them. Push the far-left square up but sit other squares right in the base of the pile, even as you migrate to the right.

Step 3. Move the 9 stacks of squares carefully to the sewing machine. Start sewing from the first row. Move gradually to the top square while the second square sits face-down on the top square. Use safety pins to join their right sides.

Step 4. Remove the pins as you sew the edge. Leave 1/4" space for seam allowance. But try to measure the printed edges of the packaged squares to know if the edge is up to the required 5 inches. Do the measurement before you start sewing the fabric. Feel free to use the valley or any edge you want to make your patchwork baby quilt. Still, if you are dealing with complex patterns, you will need to watch out for the correct edge.

Again, make sure that your seam allowance is consistent. The standard seam allowance for all quilt designs is 1/4". Always stick to this standard if you don't want to mess up your design.

Step 5. Make square 3 face square 2 and pin them together. Sew them 1/4" off the edge as you remove the pins.

Step 6. Continue sewing to add the other 6 blocks to the rows' right side. Start the process all over again to perfect all the 9 rows.

Step 7. Arrange your seams to one side without opening them. Seams should be pressed to one side when you are making a quilt so that they don't split open. Pressing these seams could be tasky but it is what you have to do to create neat and beautiful quilts.

Press the seams to your left if your rows have odd numbers. But, should you have even-numbered rows, press your seams to the right. With this, you can sew and join rows quickly and easily too. Again, turn over the seams and press them from up downward to keep them flat and nice.

Step 8. Sew the rows, make row 1 and 2 face each other, match the seams, and butt up the pressed seams, one against the other. Sew everything together and leave 1/4"space for seam allowance.

Don't sew the rows, one after the other, in a big section because it could mess up your work. Instead, pair the rows and sew them. Freely use pairs such as 1 &2, 3 &4, 5 & 6 until the numbers of your rows terminate. Sew the pairs to create a section of rows of two halves. Sew the halves to have a whole. With this method, you can easily manage your work and create great quilts in no distant time. Also, since the row seams will be in one direction, pressing becomes so easy. You only need to press the seams from the front to keep them flat and open.

How to Finish Your Patchwork Baby Quilt

You're done with the quilt top. Great work so far! What's next? Add your backing and batting layers first, baste them, and feel the beauty of your baby quilt. How can I choose the right batting for my quilt?

Factors to Consider Before You Choose Batting for a Quilt

Loft and fiber are two major factors you need to consider before you choose your batting.

1. **Loft**: How thin or which is the batting? You could have a low loft and high loft batting. Low loft means thin while high loft symbolizes thick. Low loft batting is less bulky but perfect for thinner quilts. It works fine with a running stitch either by hand or on home machines. So, consider using low loft batting for your do-it-yourself quilting. Use high loft batting for thicker projects.

2. **Fiber**: What's the batting made from? Don't use batting if you don't know its source. Polyester, Cotton or Poly Blend, and 100% Cotton are the three major types of quilt batting. Each of these batting types has its merits and demerits. Recently, Bamboo, Silk, and Wool, being natural batting options, flood the market. These natural

batting options come with wonderful qualities but they are very expensive.

- Polyester: Polyester is durable and less expensive. It has amazing low loft options for hand-quilting.Its high loft options can make your quilting unique and it is good for anyone who wants to design thicker quilts.Polyester comes with warmer batting options and it provides insulation without extra weight. However, polyester shifts a lot even when quilting is not dense. In other words, polyester fibers often leave the fabric for the exterior part of the quilt.

- Cotton: Cotton is a thick, light, and natural fiber. Its heavy weight makes it a perfect for machine quilting. Cotton washes easily and it doesn't pill. The 100% cotton shrinks slightly when quilting with it but this could be good or bad for you, depending on your quilting goal. After the first wash, I love to see my batting shrink. Why? It gives the quilt a vintage appearance and also softens it.

- Cotton Blend: Cotton blend is made up of 80 percent cotton and 20 percent polyester. It is a cotton lookalike and it rarely shrinks although it is less expensive. Cotton blend works fine with machine quilting and it is what many intermediate quilters use.

- Wool: Wool is one hundred percent natural fiber but it shrinks a lot. Don't jump at it unless you get some assurances that it will work fine for your project. Pay keen attention to the label to know whether it is pre-shrunk or not. Wool tends to resist folding and creasing but it works fine with fancy stitching and quilting. Again, wool makes hand-quilting a whole lot of fun. Wool batting is lighter-weight and warmer but very expensive. Again, wool could trigger allergic reactions in certain individuals.

- Bamboo: Bamboo is eco-friendly and a natural fiber. It aids breath ability since it is blended with Cotton. Quilts made with Bamboo batting usually come with amazing texture. Bamboo batting works fine with machine-quilted quilts.

- Fusible Batting: Fusible batting has fusible resin on its two sides. With this resin in place, you don't have to stress yourself to baste your quilt. Just iron the three layers at once if you want to baste the quilt. Sure, being a temporary fusing method, you can trust fusible batting when you are working on small scale quilts.

Be sure that the four sides of your quilt backing is bigger than your design. Press your quilt backing, spread it face-down on a surface, center your batting on it, and lower your quilt top face-up on it. Still, don't baste until you are able to see the three layers clearly from the top. Remember quilting starts from the top of your quilt. So, feel free to slightly shift the backing and batting as you deem fit.

Chapter Summary

- Baby quilts are charming, beautiful, and adorable artworks every child would like.

- The rainbow baby quilt has the radiant colors of a rainbow but you need a bit of creativity to design it.

You just designed a few colorful baby quilts. Great. In the next chapter, you will learn how to design paisley on a quilt.

Chapter Five:
Paisley on Quilt

Paisley looks charming and attractive on every quilt but very difficult to design. Still, paisley on quilt is one design you'll love to create right there in your home. Here is a fun project of a quilt designed with paisley. No worries, I will explain the process step-by-step so that you can start it straight away.

Required Materials

- An existing quilt (be it a baby quilt or a full-size quilt) or simple create a new one.

- Threads (based on your fabric)

- Needle (based on your thread)

- Gloves

- Quilting machine

Instructions

Follow these simple steps to design your own paisley on quilt project.

Step 1. Thread and needle your machine. Feel free to sketch the pattern of the quilt you want to design with chalk.

Step 2. Place your quilt below the needle and begin quilting.

Step 3. Sketch out the boundaries, secure the stitches, and create the design.

Step 4. Rotate the machine to make the needle run through your quilt. Make sure the quilt can move freely.

Step 5. Keep quilting to complete the design and secure your stitches.

Step 6. Double-stitch the edge of the quilt and trim excess fabric or thread.

How to Create a Pleasing Paisley on Quilt Pattern

Here is a beautiful paisley on quilt pattern that you can quilt with a machine or hand. Just make sure you complete the piercing and appliqué before you quilt the highly decorative paisley on quilt pattern. Here is how to design it.

Required Materials

- 36" mottled white

- 9" green print

- 36" mottled gold

- 7/8 yard teal print

- 9" gold print

- 51" square batting

- Monofilament thread (clear)

- 76" backing fabric

- Fusible web (lightweight)

- Scraps of pink and light teal print

Instructions

Follow these simple steps to design a paisley quilt pattern.

Step 1. Download your favorite paisley on quilt patterns online.

Step 2. Spread a fusible web over your pattern, paper side up. Trace the lines of each pattern with a pencil, leave 1/2" between the tracings, and cut out the fusible-web shapes, 1/4" away from traced lines.

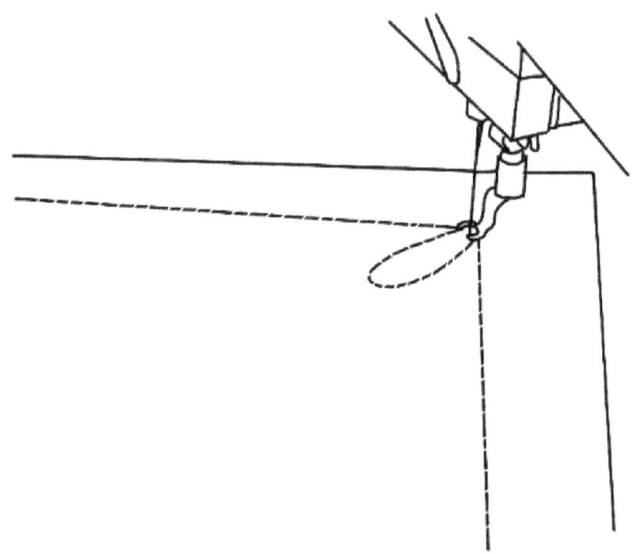

Step 3. Press fusible-web shapes on designated fabrics but follow the manufacturer's instructions. Let it cool down before you knit cut-out fabric shapes on drawn lines, or trim paper backings.

Cut 1" by 31" square from the mottled white for the center of the quilt. From the green print, cut four 2" by 33" strips for the inner border, three 2" by 31" inner border strips, and 13 Pattern D. Use the mottled gold to cut three 2" by 2" middle border strips and four 2" by 33" middle border strips.

Cut four 5" by 42" binding strips, five 1" by 4" diagonal squares, 9 Pattern A, and three 2" by 8" diagonal triangles from the teal print. Also, from the gold print, cut 9 Pattern B, 15 Pattern C, and 9 Pattern D, even as 12 Pattern E from the light teal print.

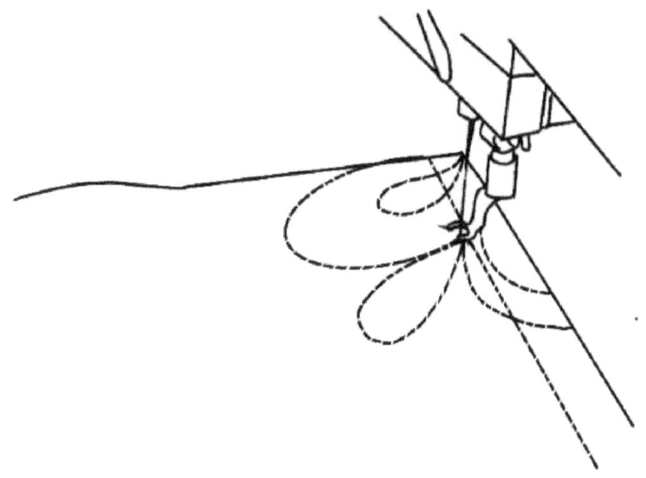

Step 4. Add inner and middle borders. Sew the opposite edges of the mottled white on the green print inner border strips, join the long green border strips to the edges, and press the seams towards the border.

Attach the middle mottled gold strips to the quilt edges before you join the long mottled gold strips to the remaining edges, and press the seams towards the border.

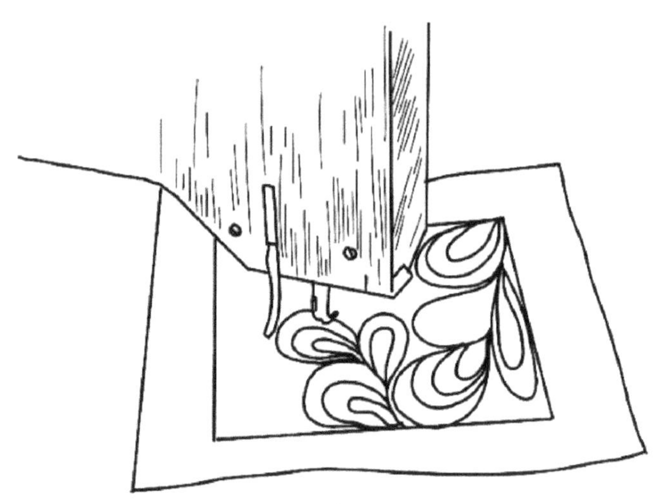

Step 5. Appliqué quilt center. Spread out the A-E appliqué pieces on the center of your quilt. Stitch the appliqué zigzag, using the clear monofilament thread on your machine.

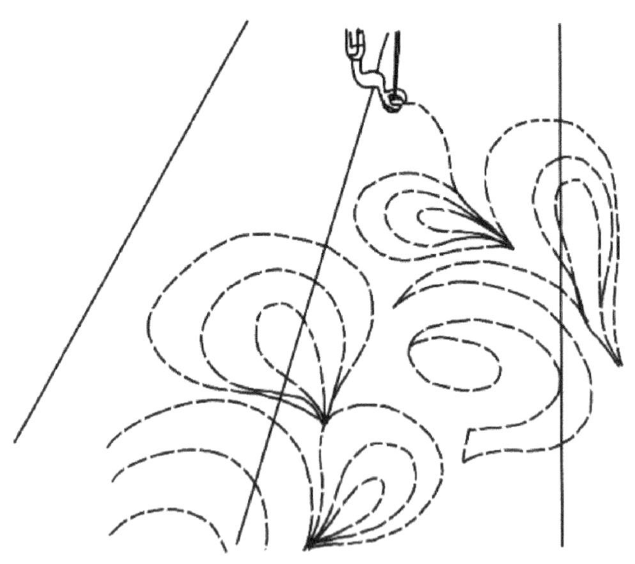

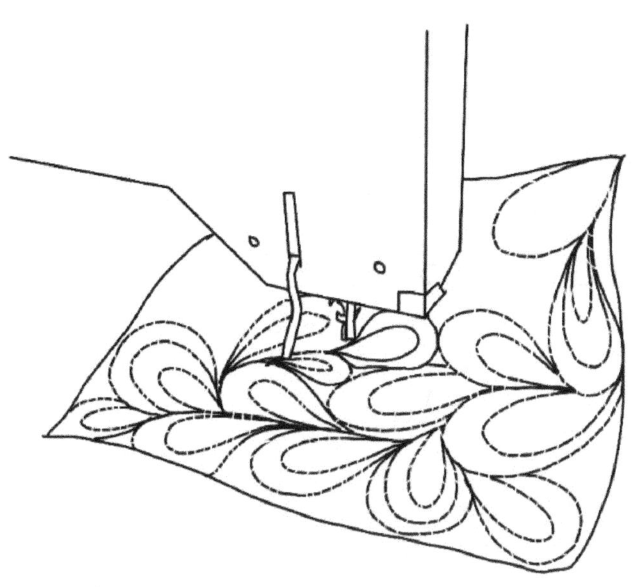

Step 6. Join the outer border. Arrange and sew the mottled gold triangles and both small and large teal print triangles, leaving 1/4" seam allowance. Press the seam to the triangle and add other large triangles, following the same process. Sew opposite exterior center edges together and press seams towards the center border.

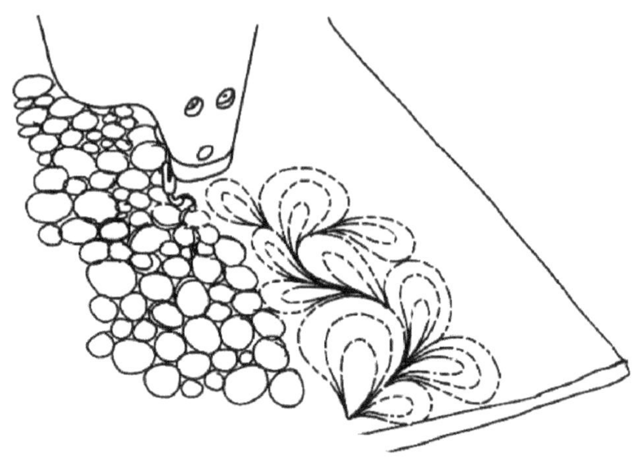

Step 7. Finish the quilt. Baste the batting, backing, and quilt top, and bind the quilt with the teal print binding strips.

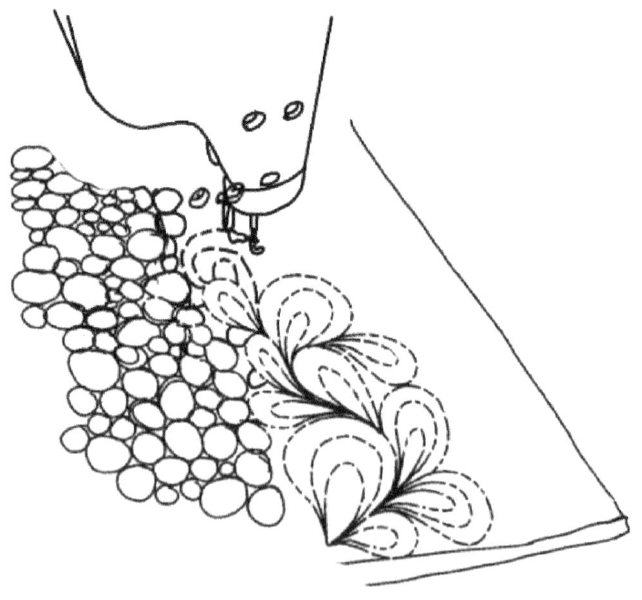

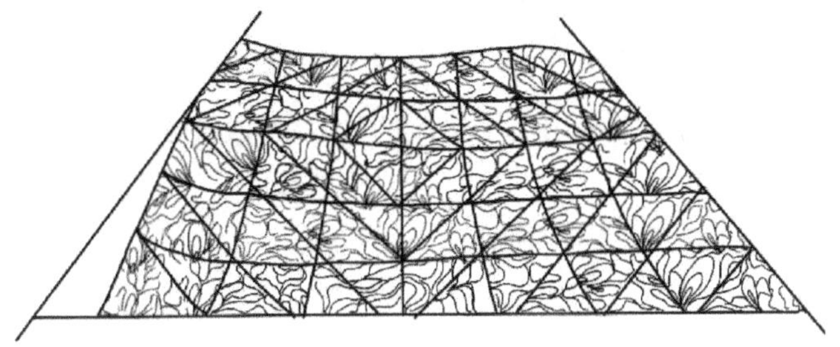

How to Design a Cotton Quilt

Here is a unique homemade quilt you can present as a gift for everyone. Again, it is a lovely quilt for babies. Sewing a Cotton quilt at the comfort of your home is personally gratifying. Use your favorite fabric and pattern to design a unique cotton quilt. Here is how to design the quilt.

Required Materials

- 46" × 54" fabric (100% cotton)

- 46" × 56" backing (100% cotton)

- 90" × 54" batting (100% cotton)

- A pair of scissors

- Bodkin

- Yarn

- Tape Measure

Instructions

Follow these simple steps to design your own cotton quilt

Step 1. Spread out the right sides of backing materials opposite each other on a surface and add the backing on either side of the materials.

Step 2. Pin all edges evenly to tack the three layers.

Step 3. Serge exterior edges of the four sides, leaving a 6" by 8" gap at the starting point, and drawing the quilt out through the gap.

Step 4. Hand-sew the gap to seal the quilt and iron the quilt to prepare it for tufting.

Step 5. Cut yarn 6 inches long, measure rug, and sew tufts 12" apart. Thread bodkin, pull it through, and tie the knot.

You just designed your own cotton quilt, congratulations.

How to Design Paisley Shorts

Sewing novices and intermediate quilters tend to find paisley shots intimidating to design. Some say that the processes are hectic while others simply believe that such projects aren't just for them. Well, with a little work and patience, you can surely design a pair of nice and comfortable elastic paisley shots at the comfort of your home. No worries. I will run you through the process of designing beautiful shots for men and women.

Paisley Shots for Women

Follow these simple steps to design a woman's paisley shot.

Step 1. Sketch your pattern: Create your pattern from the scratch or trace an outline on a piece of drawing or craft paper to save time. Here's how to trace a pair of shots.

- Fold the shorts in half but ensure that front pockets stay outside while you trace the outline on a craft paper.

- Create 1 inch seam allowance at the sides and bottom of the pattern.

- Create 4 cm space for the waistband at the top of the pattern and use scissors to cut out the pattern.

Step 2. Pin the pattern to your fabric: Fold the fabric in half, spread the pattern on it, and pin both together. Just make sure that the center part of the pattern rests directly on the fabric's folded edge. Still, to get the whole thing done accurately, sketch the pattern on your fabric before you cut it.

Step 3. Cut the fabric: Carefully cut the fabric along the outline with sharp sewing shears to get the shots' one full side. Repeat the process to create the second full side of your shots. Lay the two pieces on a surface but ensure that the right sides face each other. Pin each piece along the rounded seams and remember that you'll still stitch the seams to align the shorts.

Step 4. Stitch the seams: Machine-sew the shorts along the seams. Use a backstitch if you want to hand-stitch the shorts. Still, leave 1" seam allowance, and you'll be left with what looks like a tube of fabric.

Step 5. Turn out the shorts: Flip out the shorts to properly sit the center back and front of the fabric. Sewn seams occupy the outside edges once you join the two pieces together. Rotate the shots to align the seams evenly and down to the center. Sewn seams will form the shorts' crotch once you complete sewing.

Step 6. Sew inner thigh seams: Flatten the fabric, pin both sides, and sew along the seams to complete each leg of the shots. Keep the 1 inch seam allowance and use a zigzag stitch to sew all the sides together. Still, make sure that the seams fall on the inner thigh.

Step 7. Create a waistband: Turn over the upper edge of your fabric to accommodate the elastic band. Pin and stitch the waistband along the edge of your fabric. Here's how to create the waistband.

- Fold the top-part of your fabric by 2" to provide space for your waistband elastic.

- Use your sewing machine to sew a straight stitch along the edge of your fabric. Feel free to backstitch with your hand.

- Create a small hole in the seam edge to run the waistband elastic.

Step 8. Run the elastic through your waistband: Pass the elastic through the hole in the seam edge to the other end of your waistband and sew the opening.

Just make sure that the size of the elastic is roughly 3 inches less than your waist. Why? Elastic must stretch if you want it to stay secure. The extra space can make the shorts secure and fit.

Pin one side of the elastic so that you can run it freely through the waistband. Pull out the two ends from the waistband before you zigzag-stitch the elastic to close the opening.

Step 9. Hem the shots: Fold each leg's bottom edge by 1 inch, pin it, and sew to design a hem around the leg. Here is how to do it.

- Create 1/2" seam allowance as you sew the hemmed part around the shots' leg opening.

- Sew the shorts' front and back separately, not together.

Paisley Shorts for Men

Paisley shorts for men are slightly different from those meant for women but you can master them in no distant time. Here's how to design paisley shorts for men.

Step 1. Download patterns online: Patterns for men paisley shorts are available online, free of charge. Print the pattern on A4 paper but leave the 'scale printing' box unchecked. Each pattern you download comes with some instructions. Make sure you abide by all the instructions as you try to cut out the patterns or tape them to their designated places.

Step 2. Pin the pattern on your fabric: Spread your fabric on a surface, with its wrong side facing up, and pin the pattern on it. Here's how to do it.

- Pin the pattern to the wrong side of the fabric. Sketch the pattern on the fabric with a sewing pencil or chalk to achieve accuracy.

- Check to see whether the pattern comes with seam allowance. Fold the fabric to form a double layer and pin the pattern to it.

Step 3. Cut out the fabric: Use sharp sewing shears to cut out each piece of the pattern from the fabric. Cut out the pieces again but in reverse order and pin the pieces together.

Step 4. Design and stitch the back pockets: Pin pocket pieces appropriately on the shorts, double-stitch pockets' top and sew the pockets' sides and bottom. Press pockets' edges with iron, create an edge for the pocket opening, double-stitch the edge, and sew the pockets to the fabric.

Step 5. Design and stitch the front pockets: Design the front pockets the way you created the back pockets. Here's how to do it.

- Press the edges of the pocket pieces with an iron.

- Double-stitch the pocket's top hem and create an opening for the pocket.

- Pin the pocket to the shorts and double-stitch its sides and bottom.

Step 6. Sew the crotch: Hold the shorts firm, pin its back portions, and sew the portions along the crotch. Here is how to complete the process.

- Hold the right sides, with each facing the other, and pin the pieces firmly.

- Shape each side of the seam to 9.5 mm with sharp sewing shears. Also, clip and curve the bottom part of your crotch seam.

- Sew up the crotch seam with a flat felled seam.

Step 7. Stitch the remaining parts of the seams: Stitch side seams— right and left sides— and the inseam, the seams within the shorts. Lock the inseam with the raw edge to avoid excess fraying as soon as you sew the inseam. Sew the side seams, using the flat felled seam technique.

Step 8. Hem the shorts: Fold up the bottom hem and hold it firmly by double-stitching the top of the hem. Use an iron to press the bottom hem to design a sturdy fold on the shorts.

Step 9. Sew the lining of the waistband: Hold the shorts, make the right sides of the waistband face each other, pin it, and sew the waistband lining down to the waist. Just line up the joint of the waistband evenly, like the middle of the back waist part.

Step 10. Join the elastic waistband: Create 1/2"overlap on the edges of the raw ends of the elastic waistband and zigzag-switch it. But make sure the elastic is shorter than the elastic waistband so that it can sit well on your waist. How can I do this? Just measure the wearer's waist round and subtract 3 inches from the measurement value. The elastic band can stretch out if you follow this process and the designed shorts will be nice on the person wearing it.

Step 11. Fold the elastic into the material: Spread the shorts on a surface, pin the elastic on it, and sew to finish the shorts. No worries. Just follow these simple steps.

- Lay shorts on a surface, with the back waist facing up. Pin the elastic in the middle of the waist.

- Turn the shorts, with the front waist facing up. Half-fold the band and pin it in the middle of the front waist.

- Divide the band into some evenly-spaced points and pin it on 8 or 10 different places on the fabric.

- Fold the edge of the lining on the elastic waistband but let the wrong side face out. Stretch the elastic gently a bit and sew straight along the edge.

- Flip the shorts to turn out the right sides. Stretch the elastic gently a bit before you double-stitch the top of the waistband.

Chapter Summary

- Paisley looks charming and attractive on every quilt but very difficult to design.

- A Cotton quilt is a beautiful and unique homemade quilt for every child.

- You need a bit of creativity and plenty of endurance to create adorable paisley on quilt projects.

The next chapter is dedicated for Strip-pieced contemporary chevron designs. Lots of things to learn there!

Chapter Six: Strip-Pieced Contemporary Chevron

Strip-pieced contemporary chevron designs are unique. Not only are they beautiful and appealing, the designs are so simple that you can create them at home. Yes, in this chapter, I will teach you how to use Strip cutouts to design a quilt with contemporary chevron. Sure, you will love this fun project and you'll want to create it your own way any time soon. Also, in this chapter, you'll see other contemporary chevron projects to design. However, let us quickly run through the first project for the day— a contemporary chevron quilt.

Required Materials

- A well-feathered quilt (make sure it has adequate space you can work with)

- Fabric strips (balanced rhapsody color).

- Rotary cutter

- Scale

- Sewing machine

Instructions

Follow these simple steps to design your own quilt with contemporary chevron.

Step 1. Scale your fabrics and use the rotary cutter to cut the fabric strips to smaller pieces.

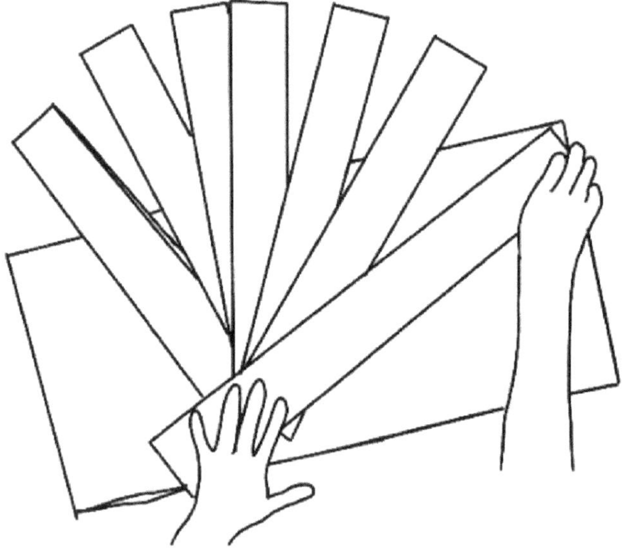

Step 2. Trim your background strips to the size of the small fabric pieces and carefully arrange the pieces. Create a few arrows that you'll work with.

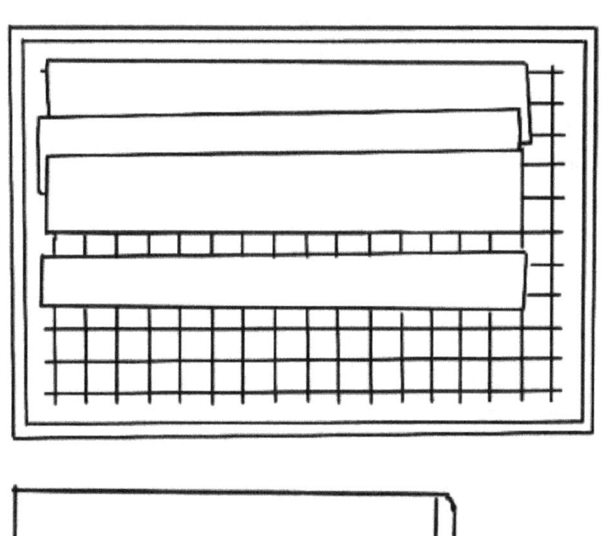

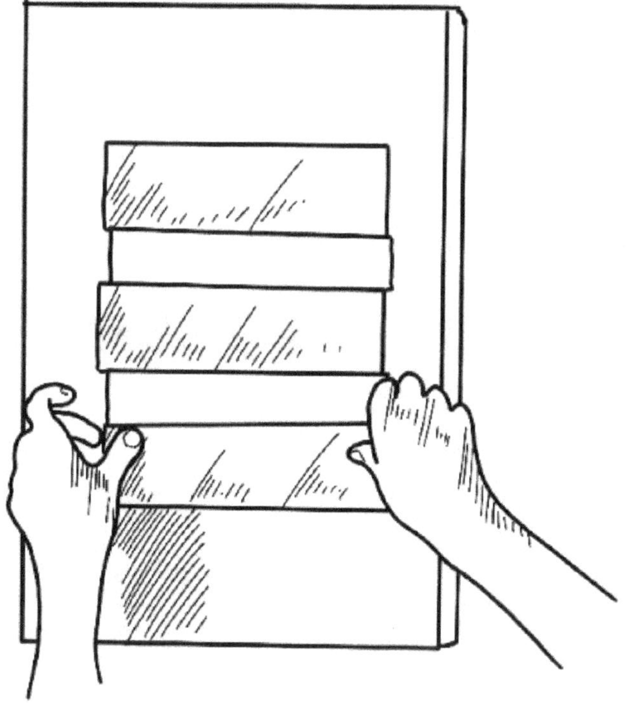

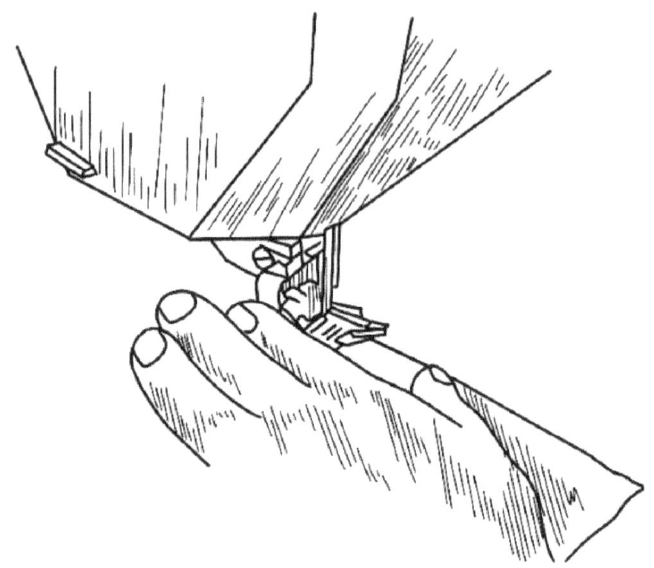

Step 3. Sew the arranged pieces together to create the first block. Heat the block with an iron to rid puckers or smoothen the block, and arrange the sewn pieces together again.

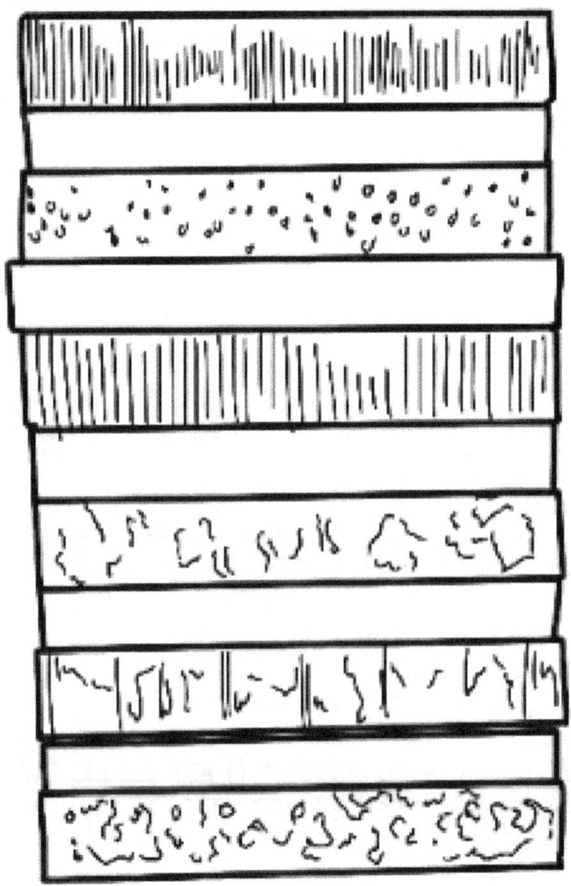

Step 4. Trim excess fabric edges until it is 45 degree. Also, trim the edges of your block to make the quilt appear neat and well-shaped.

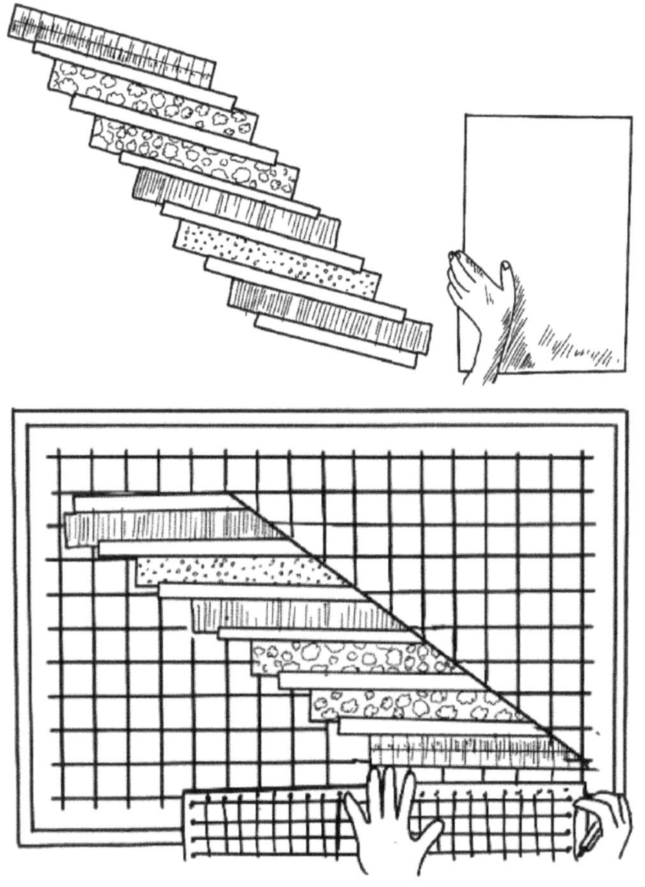

Step 5. Repeat steps 3 and 4 until you use all the pieces to create pattern blocks. Rotate the fabric but vary its directions, and design the pattern on your quilt.

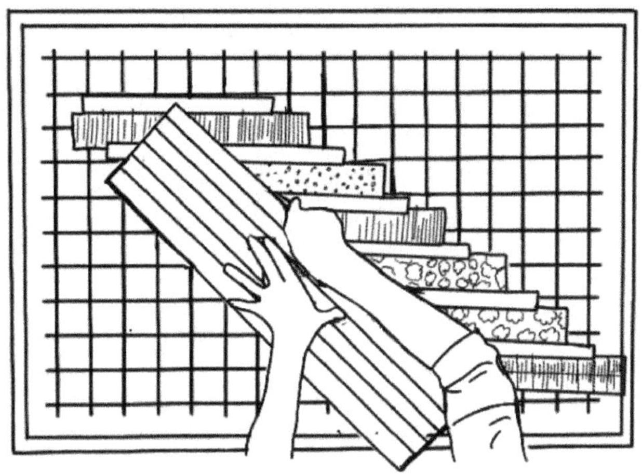

Step 6. Lay the pattern on your quilt and start quilting, one pattern before the other.

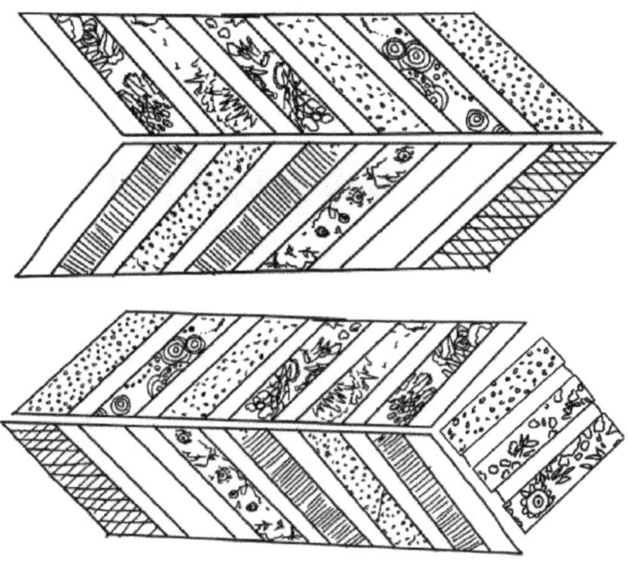

Step 7. Stitch the edges to secure the quilt.

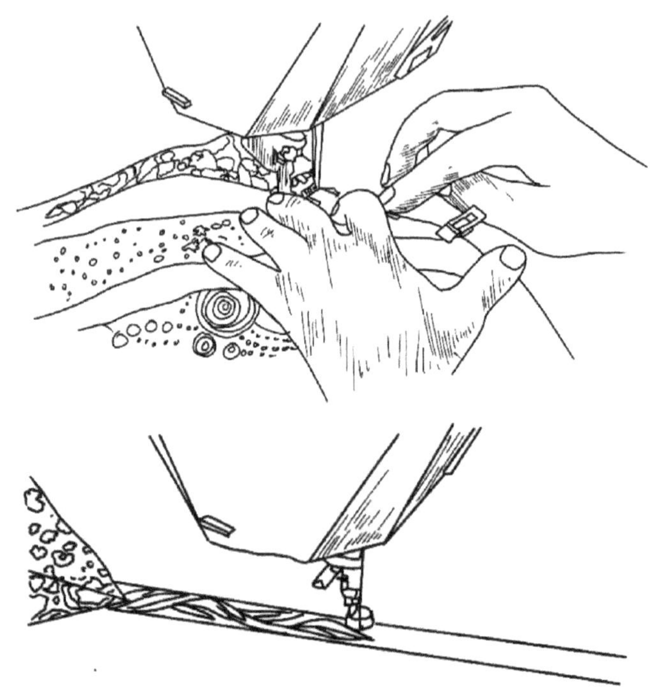

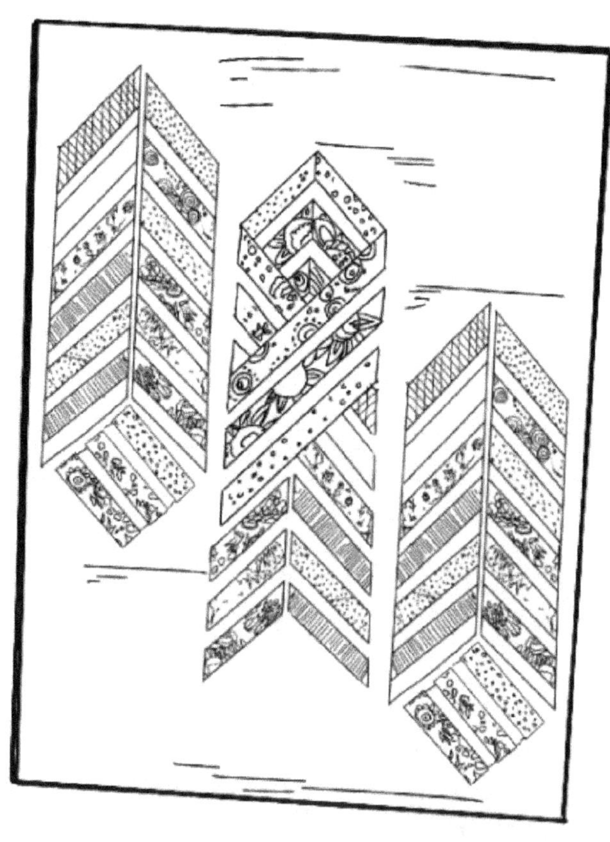

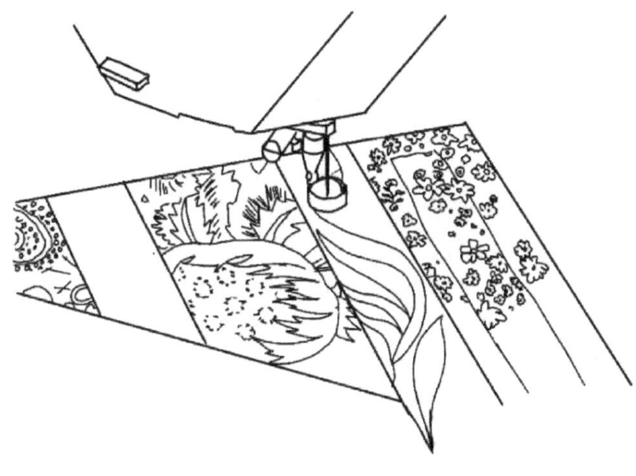

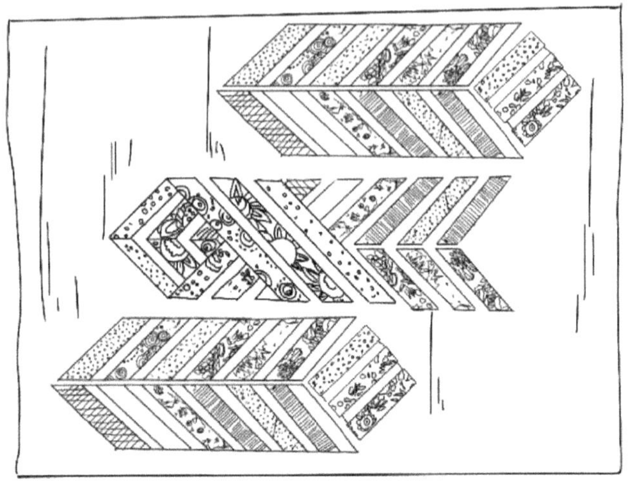

Feel free to show off your awesome project.

How to Design a Bandana Bracelet

Bracelets look good and most people, especially kids, love them. A bandana bracelet is just like other bravelets— very easy to design. Just a few tricks and you'll be on your way to design your first bandana bracelet. Here is how you can design it right there in your home.

Required Materials

- Fabric strips

- Lollipop sticks

- Hot glue

- Fish tank tubing

Instructions

Follow these simple steps to create your own bandana bracelet.

Step 1. Cut the fabric to a few 1 inch strips and remove the strings.

Step 2. Cut tubing to your size, or the size of the person you want to design it for, and cut lollipop sticks to small pieces or chunks. Put some hot glue on each side of the tube and insert the lollipop stick to form a small circle. Don't add the glue on the two ends at a time. No. It has to be one after the other.

Step 3. Add some hot glue to the hem of the fabric to gum it to the tube. Muffle the fabric all over the tube. Feel free to twist the fabric when there's need.

Step 4. Continue the process until you cover the tube with fabric completely.

A 22" bandana strip is enough to create a bracelet for a small child. But, should you run out of fabric in the process, splash a little glue on another strip, and roll it over the tube. Still, you'll need to muffle extra strips of fabric to fill up the seams.

Step 5. Trim excess fabric and add more glue to secure the bracelet.

How to Design a 5 Inch Fabric Flower

Consider spicing up your dressing with the 5 inch fabric flower. It is bold, beautiful, attractive, and charming, and it'll surely give you a unique look each time you wear a dress adorned with this lovely design. Still, you can give it out to someone who means the world to you. How can I create it? No worries. I am going to show you how you can design your own 5 inch fabric flower straight away.

Required Materials

- 23" by 3.25" fabric scrap

- A pair of scissors

- Needle and thread

- Marker

- Template

- Tiny piece of felt

Instructions

Follow these simple steps to design your own 5 inch fabric flower

Step 1. Download a template online to get started. But, if you already have one to use, fine. Place the template on the wrong side of your fabric, trace it with a marker, and sketch 9 or more petals on the fabric.

Step 2. Carefully use the scissors to cut the pattern out. Slip a thread into your normal hand needle and hem the lower edge of your fabric.

Step 3. Sew the fabric ends together to form the shape of a flower and stitch the center of the fabric to hold or secure the flower.

Step 4. Adorn the flower with a button or add other lovely embellishments.

So cute, isn't it?

How to Design a Herringbone Quilt

Herringbone quilts look appealing, beautiful, and charming, but difficult to design for some quilters. Still, you can successfully design it in your home. Just follow these simple steps to design a homemade Herringbone quilt.

Required Materials

- Quilting fabric (different colors)

- Thread

- Batting

- Ruler

- Cutting mat

- Rotary Cutter

- Sewing machine

- Safety pins

Instructions

Follow these simple steps to create your own Herringbone quilt.

Step 1. Cut the fabric to 42" by 63" blanket size. Don't forget that the quilt combines some chevrons of four squares each and each square has two triangles. Feel free to alter the squares to suit your favorite dimension. Cut 8" by 8" squares of fabric for the triangles. Fold the squares in half and cut diagonally. Repeat the process until your triangles are enough for the quilt.

Still, you can make each chevron unique and different. Just cut 8" square from each fabric, fold in half to have 4 triangles. Also, ready twenty seven 8" squares gray fabric.

Step 2. Join the fabric pieces. With right sides facing each other, sew one colored triangle with a gray one but leave 1/4" seam allowance. Press-iron the seam, clip extra fabric, and repeat the process till you have 54 squares for the quilt.

Arrange and rotate the squares till you use the colored fabric to form a 'V' shape. Fold the two squares, one on the other, but allow their right sides to face each other. Line the corners equally, sew along the edges, but don't forget to leave the 1/4" seam allowance. Iron the edges of the seam to keep it flat.

Use the same process for the remaining 2 squares. Join the top and bottom edges of the chevron. Line up the center seam before the join the pieces together, and iron the edges of the seam once you sew the pieces. Pin chevron columns to the point where the seams intersect but align columns' tip with the tip of the seams. Join all the columns and iron the seams flat. Don't drag the iron on the fabric. Instead, raise it and place it on the part you want to press. You just finished the quilt top.

Step 3. Design the quilt sandwich. Spread the backing on a surface, right side facing down, and smoothen the batting on it. Spread the quilt top on it, right side facing up, and pin everything on each triangle firmly.

Step 4. Quilt along the top of the seam till you sew the whole quilt.

Step 5. Bind the quilt. Trim excess batting and backing, but feel free to leave extra 1/4" batting if you love a fuller binding. Sew dyed colored fabric scraps to bind the quilt, muffle some along the Quilt's perimeter, and iron-press the quilt.

You have just designed a Herringbone quilt, congratulations.

How to Create a Zigzag Quilt Pattern

A zigzag quilt pattern is very unique but it requires a little bit of creativity. Visualize how you really want it to look like before you start quilting the pattern. Here is how you can design your special zig zag quilt pattern right there in your home.

Required Materials

- 5" square charms (150)

- 36" border fabric

- 18" binding fabric

- 62" by 72" batting

- 144" backing fabric

- Iron

- Sewing machine

- Safety pins

Instructions

Follow these simple steps to design your own zig zag quilt pattern

Step 1. Trim off the selvages from the border fabric. Cut out eight 4 1/2 inch strips from the fabric. Cut the square charms and batting as shown in the 'Required Materials.'

Step 2. Sew right sides of the squares together but maintain the 1/4" seam allowance. Don't forget that you are to sew the squares in rows. Use iron to press the seams on all the rows.

Step 3. Sew together rows 1 and 2; 3 and 4; 5 and 6, till you finish sewing all the 14 rows. Sew the combined rows to assemble the quilt top, and use iron to flatten the seams.

Step 4. Join the end of the border pieces until it is an 80" piece. Repeat the process to join the remaining 6 border pieces.

Step 5. Spread the quilt top on a surface, line the first border piece over the edge of the top, pin, and sew them together. Cut the lower edge of the border to make it equal with the quilt-top bottom.

Step 6. Line the second border piece over the quilt-top bottom, pin, and sew them together. Trim the border to equal it to the size of the quilt.

Step 7. Repeat the process to join other border pieces on the top and sides of the quilt. Flatten the seams again with your iron.

Step 8. Spread the backing piece, wrong side up. Lay the batting on it, and the quilt top will follow, wrong side on the batting. Baste and quilt.

Step 9. Bind the quilt with straight or bias binding.

How to Create Fabric Pumpkins

Only a look at fabric pumpkins is satisfying and fun. Should we talk about the glowing colors of the design or the multiple eyes queueing to catch a glimpse of the person using the fabric? Sure, you too can create the design. Yes, creativity is key but you will also need the tips here.

Required Materials

- Pillow stuffing

- Fabric (orange, purple, and stripe colors)

- Needle

- Thread

- A ruler

- A pair of scissors

- hot glue

- Sewing machine

* Fabric or felt (for stem and leaves)

* Basting stitch

* Twine or string

Instructions

Follow these simple steps to design your own fabric pumpkin

Step 1. Cut fabric to rectangular shapes. Vary the dimensions so that the shapes can be a little bit different from one another. Just remember that the width of a regular pumpkin is twice its height. Still, feel free to cut your fabric to many shapes so far each shape complements the other. You may cut your fabric according to this pattern.

* Orange fabric: 15.5" by 7.5" strips.

* Purple fabric: 32" by 13" strips.

* Stripe fabric: 21" by 16" strips.

Step 2. Hold the right sides of the fabric together, fold it in half, and sew with hand or machine, or put little hot glue on the side of the seam.

Step 3. Sew the lower part of the fabric pumpkin. Use your hand to sew a wide basting and join it with the pumpkin's bottom. Lift the pumpkin's bottom a bit to see if it is tightly sewn. Stitch it a few times to firmly hold or secure it.

Step 4. Turn out the right side of the fabric pumpkin, stuff it, and close its top side very well. Yet, you may need to conserve your stuffing. How? Hold the center of your stuffing and make a small hole there. Put fabric scraps or plastic bags in the hole first before you place your stuffing on it.

Step 5. Sew your basting stitch on the stuffing and seal it up, just like you closed the fabric pumpkin bottom. Close the top and stitch it a few times to firmly hold or secure the basting.

Step 6. Add finishing touches. Muffle the string or twine all over the pumpkin three or four times, or as many times as you want. Just make sure it is very tight and the tying should terminate in the fabric pumpkin's bottom. Should the bottom knot worry you, shape a felt or fabric into a circle, sprinkle little hot glue under it, and place it on the knot.

Still, feel free to add a few leaves and stems to embellish your design. Use the hot glue to attach any embellishment you want.

Herringbone Baby Quilt Pattern

Regular baby quilts look simple and beautiful, just like our quilt pattern for today, the Herringbone baby quilt. Again, this pattern blends well with most modern baby quilts. Maybe there's an expectant mum in your place and you've been wondering what to give the baby when it finally arrives, here is the

Herringbone baby quilt pattern. You don't know how to create it? No worries. Here's the how.

Required Materials

- 63" fabric A

- 63" fabric B

- 63" fabric (pink elephant for quilt back)

- 13 1/2" fabric for binding

- 40" by 60" quilt batting

- Safety pins

- Rotary cutter

- Ruler

- Sewing machine

Instructions

Follow these simple steps to design your own Herringbone baby quilt pattern.

Step 1. Cut Fabric A and B to 13.75" by 13.75" (seven pieces each).

Step 2. Mark the fabric by sketching a diagonal 'X' on all the wrong sides of the fabric's lightest pieces.

Step 3. Place one marked square of fabric A on one square of Fabric B, with right sides facing each other, and pin the two together.

Step 4. Repeat the process till you pin fabric A and fabric B squares.

Step 5. Adjust the foot of your sewing machine to set seam allowance to 1/4" and stitch either side of the pinned layers of fabric.

Step 6. Evenly divide the squares to 4 parts and cut the layers with your rotary cutter to have 8 smaller pieces. Sew the edges of the pieces and trim excess pieces.

It was simple running the steps. Yes, and you just designed a Herringbone baby quilt pattern.

How to Design a Bandana Quilt

Here is a rare but beautiful quilt you can design and complete at the comfort of your home in only a few hours. A bandana quilt is a perfect gift for anyone you truly value, and it is very simple to create. All you need to do to create this quilt is follow the instructions here.

Required Materials

- Quilt batting

- Red, white, and blue bandana

- A pair of scissors

- Ruler

- Sewing machine

- Threads

- Safety pins

- A pressing iron

Instructions

Follow these simple steps to design your own bandana quilt.

Step 1. Spread the bandana to create your favorite bandana pattern.

Step 2. Arrange the bandanas, clipping their right sides together. Leave 1/4" seam allowance and sew the bandanas along their edges. Just sow everything in a row. And, later on, pick all the rows and sew them together. However, don't try to perfectly align the edges of the bandanas or match up their corners. There's no way you can have a straight bandana.

Step 3. Repeat the above processes to perfect the other side of your quilt.

Step 4. Flatten the seams by pressing them with iron.

Step 5. Spread the quilt on a surface, wrong side facing up. Lay the quilt batting on it, trim the batting to fit the quilt, but make sure that the quilt sides are at least 3 inches more than the batting. Why? Bandana or batting may shake in the process of quilting.

Step 6. Pin the quilt batting, sew a few lines to firmly hold the quilt and batting, and remove the safety pins.

Step 7. Lay the quilt on a surface, batting side facing down, and spread the second quilt on it, wrong side facing up, to design the quilt sandwich.

Step 8. Leave an opening of 10 inches where you'll flip out the right side of the quilt. Sew everything together, only on the edges.

Step 9. Trim the excess fabric on be edges and turn out the right side of the quilt.

Step 10. Hand-stitch or use a machine to sew the 10 inches' opening and flatten the edges with iron.

Step 11. Quilt a few lines to firmly hold the front and back sides of the quilt.

Here you are. You just designed a bandana quilt.

Chapter Summary

- Strip-pieced contemporary chevron designs are appealing and simple to design but you have to be creative.

- A bandana bracelet looks perfect on many people and you can vary the design as you want.

In the next chapter you will learn how to create shattered frame quilts.

Chapter Seven:
Shattered Frame Quilt

Shattered frame quilts are beautiful, appealing, and easy to design. Again, you don't need lots of fabric to create one. There are lots of free patterns online that you can download to get started. To create one, you'll need to randomly stitch a few 2 1/2" strips together and trim them down a bit. No worries. In this chapter, I will teach you how to create a quilt and design it with a shattered frame. Also, you'll learn how to design some other quilts. But, before then, let's create a shattered-frame designed quilt. Here's how to design it.

Required Materials

- Fabrics (suitable for a quilt sandwich)

- Threads

- Needle (according to threads)

- Fabric scraps

- Sewing machine

- A pair of scissors

Instructions

Follow these simple steps to design your quilt with a shattered frame.

Step 1. Ready your scrap fabrics by cutting them into small strips.

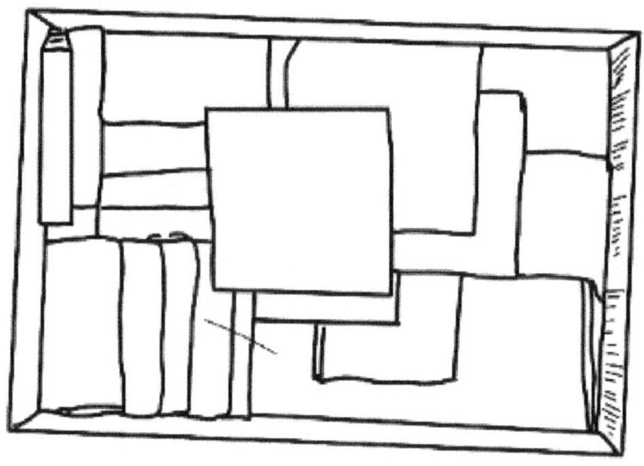

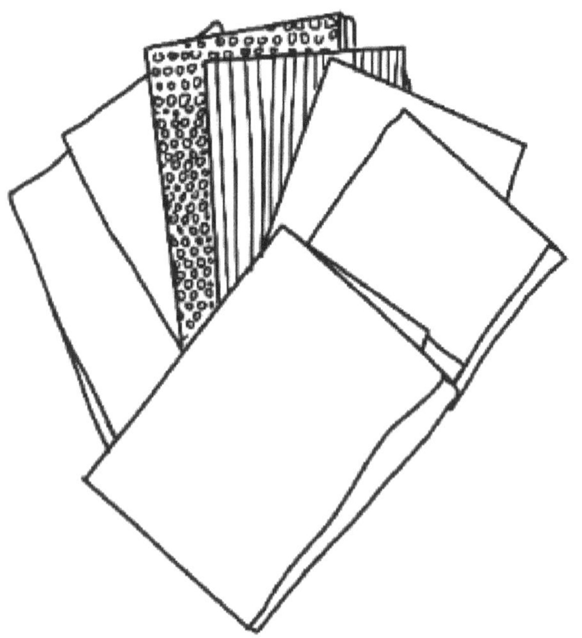

Step 2. Thread and needle your sewing machine.

Step 3. Carefully arrange the strips and stitch then from one corner to the other.

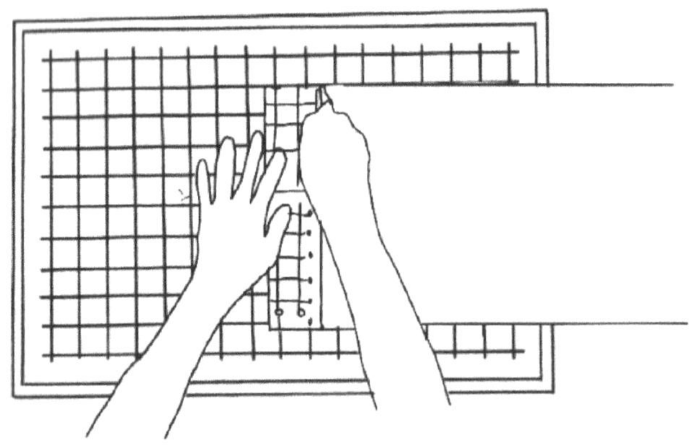

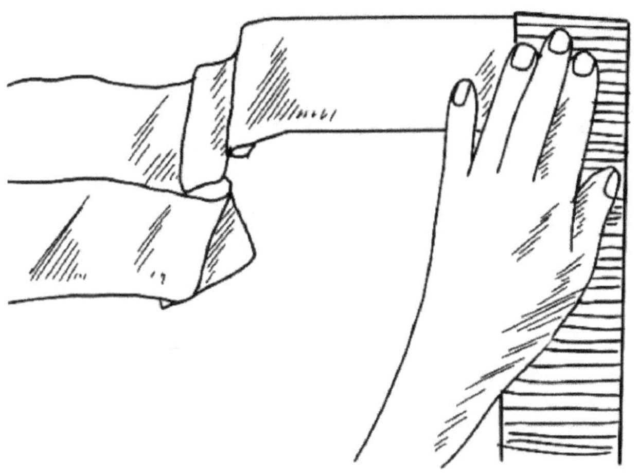

Step 4. Use the scissors to trim the edges of the strips. Turn out the strip to join 2 strips together.

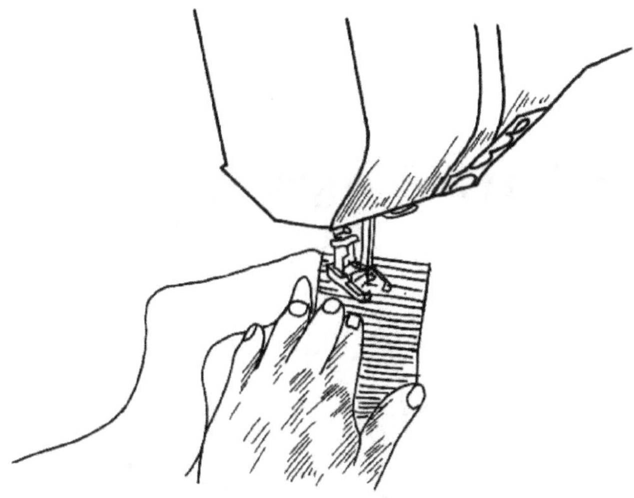

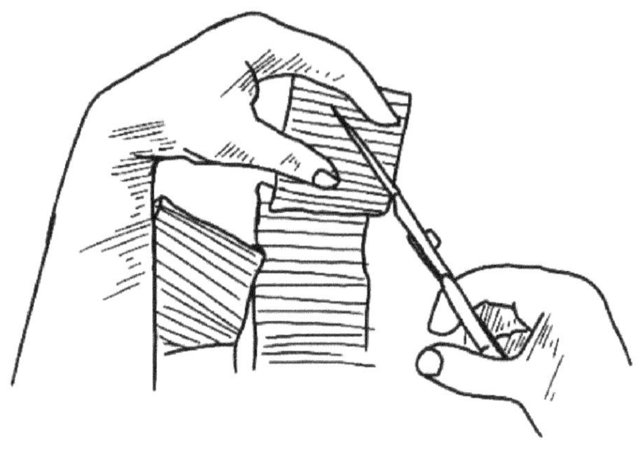

Step 5. Spread your fabric on a surface. Cut a square piece from it. Use the piece as your centerpiece.

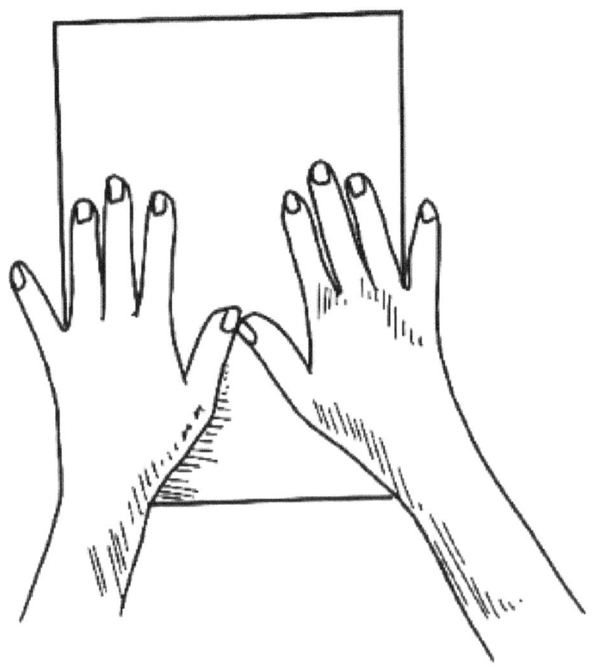

Step 6. Line up the joined strips all over the edges of the center peace. Shape them with the centerpiece to smoothen the quilt.

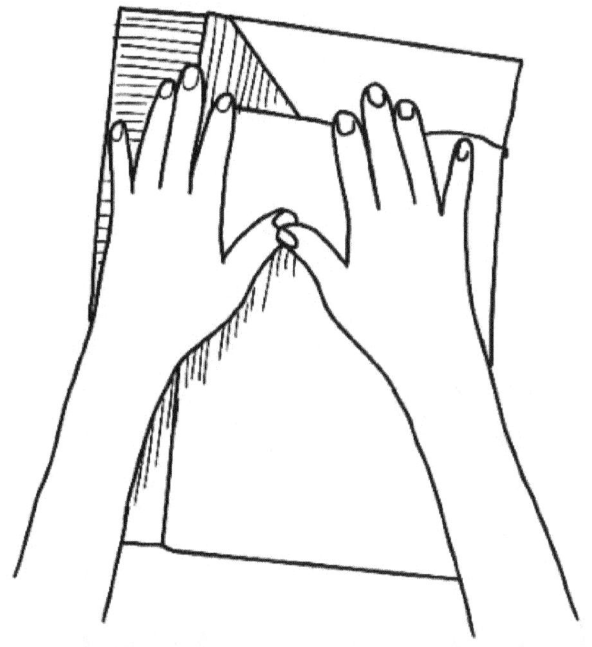

Step 7. Sew the strips together along the edges. Consider using a walking foot if you want better results.

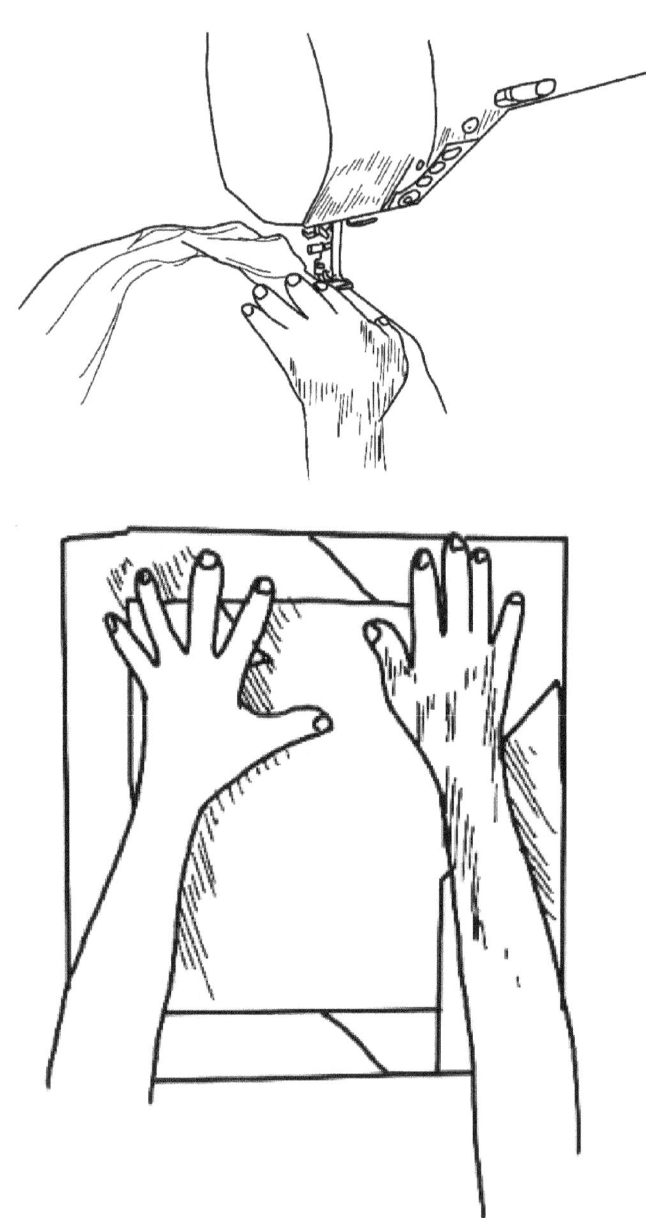

Step 8. Repeat the process continually to get the required number of rings all over the centerpiece, and ready the quilt sandwich.

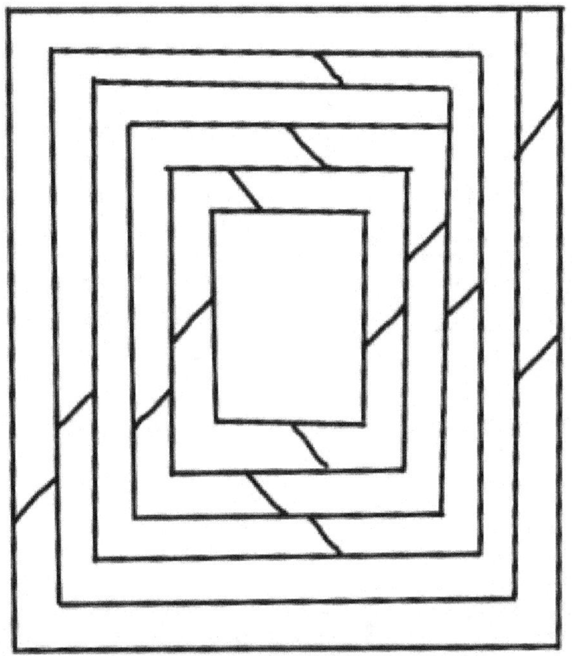

Step 9. Quilt the edges to firmly secure and hold the quilt. Join your shattered frame to the quilt.

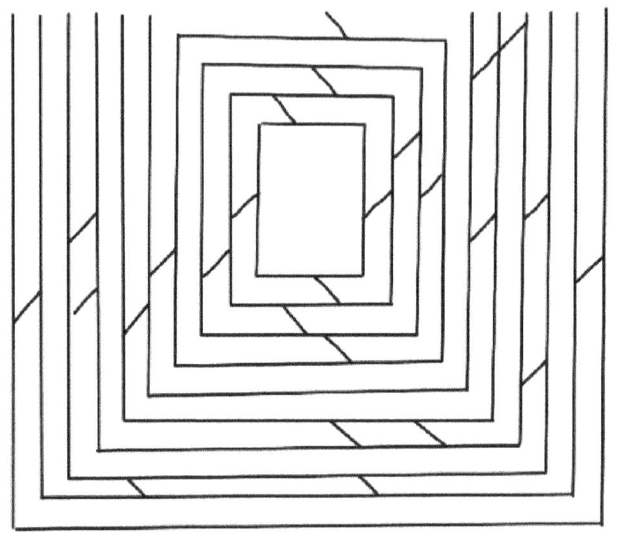

Step 10. Draw additional patterns to fill the negative space. You may download patterns if you can't create one from the scratch.

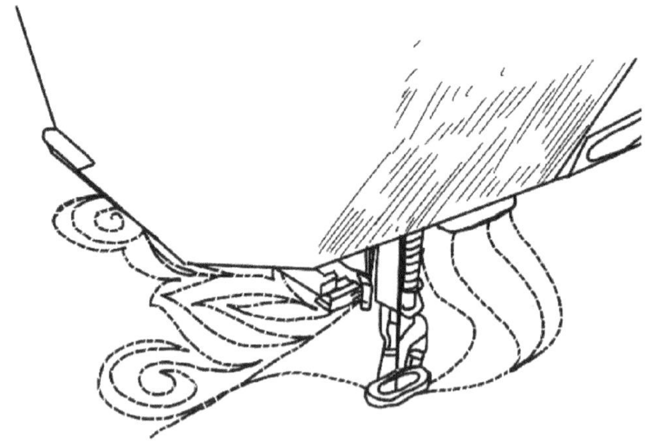

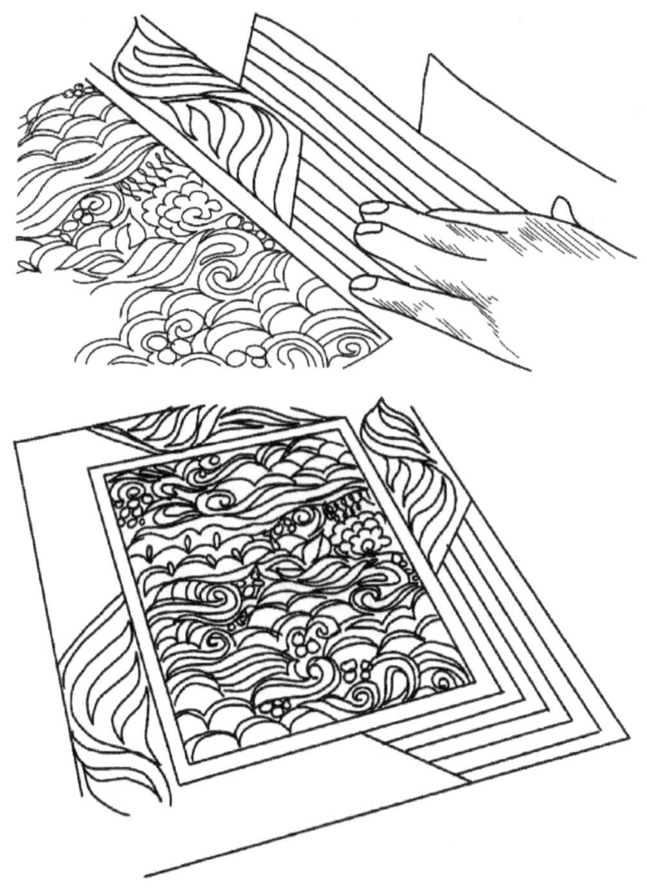

Here you are. You just designed a custom-made quilt.

How to Design a Baby Blanket

I already told you that you don't need lots of fabric to create beautiful shattered-frame quilts. Here is a lovely baby quilt that you can design with just 2 yards of fabric. Yes, creating a well-fitted baby quilt isn't always easy but you'll have no problem getting this right. I will teach you how to design this cute quilt at the comfort of your home. Use any fabric with baby-friendly colors to design this quilt and you'll surely love it. Here's how to design the blanket.

Required Materials

- 36" fabric (panel pink mixed with gold sparkle)

- 36" fabric (little fruit white)

- Thread

- Needle (according to thread)

- A pair of scissors

- 36" high loft batting

- Sewing machine

- Safety pins

Instructions

Follow these simple steps to design your own baby blanket.

Step 1. Spread your fabric on a flat surface and cut the selvage edges. Carefully trim the edges until equal size is attained.

Step 2. Shape the batting to 44" by 36" or the size of your panel. Pin the batting to the wrong side of one fabric before you attach the other fabric, but make sure their right sides stay together.

Step 3. Sew around the edges of the fabric but leave 1/2" for seam allowance. Still, create an opening of about five inches to pull out the right side of the fabric. Just make sure you trim the corners of the blanket before this is done.

Step 4. Flip the right side out through the opening, and press the blanket to straighten the edges. Pin the opening.

Step 5. Stitch the top of the opening to close it. Also sew around the edge of the blanket, leaving out the 1/4" seam allowance.

Step 6. Top-stitch the quilt over the panel boxes to arrange the layers together and attain a more lofty appearance. Do it until the whole thing turns to what you want. Backstitch and cut excess threads.

You just designed your beautiful baby blanket.

How to Create a Crazy Quilt Pattern

Crazy quilts are colorful and fun to design. They are adorable quilts you can design from home with just fabric scraps. Still, with creativity at its peak, you can alter the pattern to make it suitable for your quilt. So, rather than throwing away the scraps of your fabric, use them to design lovely crazy quilts. You don't know how to design a crazy quilt pattern? No worries, that's why I am here.

Required Materials

- Quilting ruler

- Cutting mat

- Rotary cutter

- Thread

- Needle (according to thread)

- A pressing iron and ironing board

- A pair of scissors

- Seam ripper

- Different sizes of fabric scraps

- Muslin

- Sewing machine

Instructions

Follow these simple steps to design your own crazy quilt pattern.

Step 1. Cut one square of muslin for your backing piece to stabilize your quilt block. Feel free to put the batting at the back of the muslin piece if you want to vary the quilt pattern.

A fabric piece at the center of the block will be amazing. Just trim the piece to create room for five different sizes with irregular angles, and roughly position the piece in the center of your backing fabric. Always make sure that the middle piece of your block is different a little bit.

Step 2. Pick the next fabric to attach to the block but make sure that its edges are straight. Still, the edges of the fabric should be as long as the middle piece. Align the edges of the fabric with the first one but make sure that the right side of the second fabric faces down before you sew them together.

Sew on a straight line along the edges, leaving 1/4" seam allowance. Don't stitch unless the first piece is shorter than the second one.

Step 3. Press the seams to ease the process and trim excess threads too. Don't forget your crazy quilt needs lots of pressing, trimming, and sewing. So, let your pressing iron, cutting mat, and iron board stay close to your sewing machine.

Step 4. Add the next pieces of fabric in the center piece left-hand side to properly align them. Just make sure the fabric is long enough to reach the other piece. It is normal for part of the first piece to show. As soon as all is set, sew the pieces together on a straight line across the edge, leaving 1/4" seam allowance.

Step 5. Slightly fold the backing a little bit from the seam and trim the excess edges. Add strips but don't cut them until you have sewn everything together. Extend the pieces across all the angles to add more 'craziness' to the quilt. Just be creative to make the quilt appealing.

Step 6. Remove stitches that do not hold your fabric backing. Use the seam ripper to do it. You won't be able to fold the backing if you fail to cut the stitches. Still, be mindful of how you remove these stitches or you'll rip the seams.

Step 7. Cover the backing piece with strips and trim the edges to balance the square and the backing fabric. Sew the block all over, 1/8" from the edge. Once this is done, sewing the blocks or securing the edges becomes very easy. Add additional blocks and sew everything together.

You just designed your own crazy quilt, congratulations.

How to Design a Snail's Trail Quilt Pattern

Here is a fun and popular quilt pattern that you can design at the comfort of your home. The snail's trail pattern has a few spiral patterns but is hard to create. No worries. With the few tips I want to share with you, nothing can stop you from creating one straight away. Still, feel free to add a few themes and colors to beautify your snail's trail quilt pattern. Here's how to design it.

Instructions

Follow these simple steps to design your own snail's trail quilt pattern.

Step 1. Sew a 1 5/8" by 42" light strip with a 1 5/8" by 42" dark strip, leaving 1/4"seam allowance. Press the seam to the direction of the dark strip and trim either end of the strip to 1 5/8" segment. Add the 1 5/8" leftover strips and sew the two segments together to form a four-patch unit. Place similar colors diagonally on either side and fan your seam allowance if you have bulky patches.

Step 2. Assemble the quilt block. Chain-piece each triangle to quickly assemble your quilt block. Try to master sewing for this project before you try to assemble your block. Still, you need to match your patchwork's midpoint. But, before this can be done, you need to fold your triangles to 2 equal halves. Cut 2 ½" squares, place the squares around the patchwork's four sides, and sew everything together, leaving 1/4" seam allowance. Press the seam allowance to the direction of the triangles.

Add 2 1/2" dark triangles to the edges of the patchwork and press the quilt. Continue to add more triangles until the pattern is perfect for your quilt. Feel free to alternate the sizes of your triangles, from small to large ones. Press your block until it measures 9 1/2" by 9 ½". Sew the block as soon as this is achieved.

Step 3. Arrange blocks in seven rows of six quilt blocks per row. Just make sure that the blocks are carefully aligned in the form of 'O' colors before you attach the quilt blocks.

Step 4. Arrange blocks on each row and sew them together. But don't forget to spread the blocks to opposite directions. You may have to press the quilt carefully to match each seam allowance.

Step 5. Join straight borders with the quilt. Inner borders should be 3 1/2" wide. Use the dark border fabric to cut your border.

Step 6. Press the quilt and use batting and backing to sandwich it. Use a hand or quilting machine to stitch the quilt. Also, cut off excess backing and batting from the edges of your quilt.

How to Design Hugs and Kisses Quilt Pattern

Hugs and Kisses quilt pattern, also known as the X's and O's, is a colorful quilt pattern you'll always want to design. It sits well as a baby quilt or other regular quilts, and it is easy to design. With a well cut-out layout and very nice shapes, you just can't wait to have this lovely quilt on your arms. Again, you're free to alter or vary the size of the quilt, as you want. Just up your level of creativity and create your favorite hugs and kisses quilt pattern. Like other quilters out there, feel free to create the quilt out of pre-cut 5-inches squares, if that works fine for the project you want to design. Also, there are hosts of colors to spice up your design. Any color that works fine for you is great but mix only colors that complement one another. Here's how to design your own hugs and kisses quilt.

Required Materials

- 5" by 5" dark squares (168)

- 2 3/4" by 2 3/4" light squares (336)

- 54" by 63" batting

- 54" by 63" backing

- Sewing machine

- Thread

- Needle (according to thread)

Instructions

Follow these simple steps to design your own hugs and kisses quilt pattern.

Step 1. Sketch a line from one end of a corner to the other till you cover all the small squares, and bring together two light squares and one dark square. Align the right sides of the light and dark squares. Just make sure you lay open their edges. Sew a seam over the line from top-right downward.

Step 2. Sew through every layer, leaving 1/4"
seam allowance. Press the right side of the light fabric
and the seam to design a triangle. Sew the next light
square with the larger dark square's opposite edge.
Use the previous strategy or method to do it. Trim the
edges to smoothen the quilt pattern.

Step 3. Repeat the process till the 168 dark
squares align with opposite sides' light triangles.
Arrange all the units in rows and sew everything
together.

Step 4. Spread the blocks in seven rows. Each
row should have just 6 quilt blocks. Carefully consider
the layout of the design to see if you like it. If you
don't, just shuffle the blocks, and see how the layout
now looks. Sew the blocks together once the layout
looks perfect for you.

Step 5. Press all seams flat and carefully join all
the rows together, align the seam intersections, and
press again.

Step 6. Carefully remove extra batting and
backing, and smoothen the edges of the quilt. Double
fold the binding and sew on a straight line across the
edges.

**How to Create Hugs and Kisses quilt with
Varied Proportions**

Feel free to vary the proportions of your X's and
O's quilts. Alternate the larger squares with a few half-

sized corner squares to vary your quilts. Just pay keen attention to the materials below if you want to design varied proportions of this lovely and appealing quilt.

Use these materials if you want to design a 36 inches by 45 inches Hugs and kisses quilt for babies.

- Batting and backing (as shown above)

- 5" by 5" dark squares (80)

- 2 1/2" by 2 1/2" light squares (160)

- 77" by 88" bed quilt (11" blocks, larger)

- 6" by 6" squares (224)

- 2 1/2" by 2 1/2" squares (448).

To alter your quilt, just add or subtract the adjustment from the height and width of your blocks. Still, eight small squares or four larger squares need to be added or subtracted, depending on what you really want to achieve. Also, one or more borders will be attached to the quilt.

How to Use Cornerstones and Sashings to Design a Straight Quilt

Sashing, a fabric strip or patchwork, splits one quilt block from the other. Each strip comes with nice squares that beautify the corners and sides of a quilt. Apart from enhancing the aesthetics of your quilt layout, sashing helps frame the quilt blocks, remove poor or unattractive patchworks, boost Quilt's dimensions, and balance blocks of different sizes within the quilt. Cornerstones, like sashings, can make your quilt appealing and attractive. No words can capture the striking effects that sashing and cornerstones will leave on your quilt. Just a few tricks and you'll design this straight quilt right there in your home. Here's the how.

Required Materials

- Fabric

- Thread

- Measuring tools

- Iron

- Sewing machine

- Cutting tools

Instructions

Follow these simple steps to design your straight quilt with sashings and cornerstones.

Step 1. Calculate the dimensions of the cornerstones and sashing to know the size of fabric you need for the project. Also, while deciding the length and width of your sashing, don't use strips that are not suitable for your quilt blocks' dimensions. Measure the width of your block and go for a one-fourth size sashing. In other words, if your quilt block is 12 inches, your sashing should be 3 inches.

Step 2. Sketch your quilt layout to know the amount of sashing strips and cornerstones to use for the project. Also, you need to decide the number of blocks on each row and the total rows of the quilt.

Step 3. Stylishly sew sashing units with the rows of the quilt. But feel free to sew them at the ends of your rows to create a striking effect, leaving 1/4" seam allowance. Press the seams to the direction of your sashing strips, and repeat the process till you assembled all the rows.

Align sashing strip ends with block ends and sew them together if they have equal lengths. But, should the lengths vary, fold the sashing to know its midpoint. Align midpoints and ends, and sew the blocks together to create a few narrow block rows.

Step 4. Press the seam allowance to the direction of the sashing but make sure you don't stretch the narrow rows. Sew every row and align your seam intersections, but don't forget to press the quilt flat.

You just created the straight quilt.

Chapter Summary

- Shattered frame quilts are unique and appealing, and you only need a few strips of fabric to create one.

- A well-fitted baby blanket is a cute quilt for every child you love, and you can easily design it right there in your home.

Next chapter captures Modern X quilt patterns. See you there!

Chapter Eight: Modern X

Quilts' layouts are changing rapidly in order to meet up with the changing demands. What used to be acceptable many years ago is paving way for new designs. Modern X quilts are bold, beautiful, and charming, but difficult to perfect. Still, they are designs you can run from the comfort of your home if you have someone to put you through. Yes, I am here to teach you how to create your own Modern X quilt straight away. Just pay keen attention to these tricks.

Required Materials

- A Plain Textile or Cloth

- A color role of pre-cut Textile or Cloth

- Needle

- Threads

- Rotary cutter

Instructions

Follow these simple steps to design your own Modern X quilt

Step 1: Cut out some shreds from your plain cloth. You will have to incise several hefty squares out of your plain cloth.

Step 2: After, you have to also incise several larger squares. Then incise those larger squares transversely in a triangular form.

Step 3: Afterward, you will constrict some selected pre-cut shreds to 2 breadths. After that, you will have to design a 36 square block using clipped and unclipped shreds

Step 4: Now design 3 sets of shreds with 2 shreds in each set. It is important to make use of plain shreds incised in any one of them

Step 5: Now sew them to design a square of 6 shreds. You have to press them to eject any crumples before you split clothes straight into 2 broad shreds.

Step 6: Design another 2 shreds like that and incise them just like the previous ones. You will organize those shreds, systematically, in couple of 6 shreds

Step 7: Stitch the shreds together to make 36 square boxes. Design another 7 square boxes. Now take 3 shreds from your pre-cut shreds clipped to 2 breadths

Step 8: Assemble them mutually with a balance of 2", sew them together, and build another 2 more of these but this time balance will be in other direction

Step 9: Cut your shed from the verge at 45 degree. Now, design another incise at 45 degree but in the opposite path. Make sure the wider side of the shred is 18 and a quarter in length exactly. Now cut one more out of that shred

How to Design a Straight Line Quilting

Straight line quilting, an amazing quilt design, requires total endurance to create. You may not be able to quilt if you skip every little detail. To achieve straight line quilt, we have made up this simple and speedy step-by-step procedure you can follow. Believe me you will not make any mistake if you can follow it meticulously. Now can we embark on the straight line quilting journey?

Required Materials

- A quilt all sandwiched

- basting

- A walking foot

- A guide bar and tape

- Quilting gloves

- High-quality needles and thread.

Instructions

Follow these simple steps to design your own straight line quilting

Step 1: Create a large room by the left side of the sewing machine to spread out the quilt.

Step 2: Start quilting in the center where there is a joint running down the quilt to allow you stitch in a straight line.

Step 3: Bend the right side of the quilt softly to ease its movement through the sewing machine.

Step 4: Start stitching quilt.

Step 5: You have to stitch the first line straight down to the middle of the quilt. Use the joint in the center as your guide. There is no particular way to stitch, you can either stitch from top cover of the right or left depending on your choice and creativity.

Step 6: Stitch neatly downward until you get to the batting at the base, then cut the thread. Afterward, increase the presser foot and tug the quilt in the direction of the presser foot until it got to the batting at the top again.

Step 7: You should not drag the quilt across the stitching machine. Try to hold the quilt with your hand and weigh the heaviness.

Step 8: Continue threading the quilting lines across the line anyhow you like but make it neat.

Step 9: You should set your guide bar to 1 1/2" away from the needle. After that, stitch from the right side of the guide bar through the left of the sewing line. You should try and skip two lines of the sewing. This will save your time and make it much faster.

Step 10: Carry on your quilting in only one line from top to bottom until you get to the edge of the quilt. The seam lines in your quilt top will help you to maintain a straight line.

Step 11: after you have quilted the line to the middle, move it to the other part of the quilt to finish the rest of the lines from base to summit.

Step 12: Now that you are done quilting, square up the sides, join it, and then you have made an attractive quilt.

Tips for Piercing Curves

Curves are charming. Although they appear complex to build, they are always very simple if only you understand the step by step of designing it. Several designers are frightened by the complexity of the curves but if you are capable of stitching a 1/4" seam. Then fear not, you should be able to stitch a very attractive curve. There is no cause for alarm, with some tips, confidence, endurance and rehearsal, you should sketch and stitch a nice curve. Now, let's try out some tips needed to stitch beautiful piercing curves.

Required Materials

- Cloth

- Rotary cutter

- A pair of scissors

- A guide bar and tape

- Sewing Machine

- Needles and thread.

Instructions

Follow these simple steps to pierce the curves.

Step 1: Thicken your cloth before cutting. The starch will not allow the sides from becoming threadbare or worn-out. It is advisable to use old plain starch on your cloth. This will make it more strong and durable.

Step 2. You should be careful with the type of prototype you follow and cut. Using a precise prototype can help you to achieve good results. It is advisable you use a rotary cutter for the straight lines and paper scissors for the curves. However, if achieving precision is your issue, it is better you contemplate picking a design with corresponding acrylic templates.

Step 3: you have to thread slowly when trimming your cloth or textile especially those one gotten from plastic models or straight from acrylic templates. But remember that you should be careful with the way you trace it. Take it gently.

You want to be as accurate as possible since you will be using the curved cut raw edges as a guide for your scant 1/4" seam. You will cut more accurate pieces when using a combination of sharp fabric scissors and a small 28mm rotary cutter. Try both and see what works best for you!

Step 4: Pin your curves. Pinning is tasking and time consuming, but the time is actually worth it if you are able to pin it neatly. To pin, you can take a convex and concave piece and spot the middle of both curved sides by bending them in the middle, unbend and place a pin at the crinkles. After this, bend the base and the upper sides to contact the middle pin, make the edges ranged, unbend and place pins at the crinkles.

Step 5: After you might have placed the marking pin, locate and pin the middle marks of curve pieces mutually. Also, you must increase pins in between to save the raw ends range. This pinning system is cumbersome but you should exercise patience, and confidence to understand it.

Step 6: Stitch gently. It is advisable you do a
stop and start method while sewing. You have to stitch
the curves slowly and be very sure that the raw ends
remain united as you go ahead with the stitch. Make
sure you stop and fine-tune the cloth to eschew
wrinkles. Also, try to always halt with the needle in
the extreme position in order to make your extension
stay put on the machine. Employ a ¼ foot presser to
get the perfect seam allowance.

Step 7: Stitch with your bowl-shaped piece on
top. Avoid crumples. You should endeavour to stop
often and use your finger to make sure your levels are
laying flat in the capacity you are about to stitch.

How to Make a Modern Barn Quilt

Here is the colourful modern barn quilt. It is
charming, gorgeous, appealing, fitting, and you can
surely design it from home. Just a few tricks and
you're on the way creating your own modern barn
quilt.

Required Materials

- Plywood

- Lumber

- Stain

- (50) 1-1/4" exterior screws

- Paint samples

- Painter's tape

- (6) 5" bolts

- 2" by 8" board

Instructions

Follow these simple steps to design own modern barn quilt

Step 1. Select Your Design and Buy Paint: In order to make a unique barn quilt, you must have a good knowledge of color. You should be able to use a refreshing and bright color palette that will help to achieve the aim of the work.

Use corresponding paint colors to the palette to be designed. Most of the producers of the paints have developed software that will assist you to get colors that match your project without considering the line of colors.

Step 2. Select and Cut Lumber: You must know that the magnitude of the barn quilt you are creating before you select the lumber. Just know that most barn quilts customarily have eight-foot squares, with small space available in the barn.

You must scale it down in order to build your quilt with a 4 by 4 piece of 1/4 plywood base, and planned 1 by 8 pine boards. Prior to cutting the plywood, make sure to dry the pine boards together, and quantify to know that the quilt could be a 50 square. I cut all boards to that length.

Step 3. Stain and Assemble: Staining is mandatory, infact, leaving your board natural is better. This allows you to test if your board can pass the test of time. Although, there is no problem if you decide to paint yours. However, if you want to stain make it transparent enough so that the grain of the wood will appear through it. After drying up your stain, turn the board over and place it on a square and put a 4 by 4 plywood on it.

Screw the plywood and the board but try as much as possible to make sure that the position of the board is maintained. You can put between 6 to 8 screws on the plywood and boards. Also, when staining your board, make sure all the ends at being painted and the sides of the 4 by 4 plywood especially those areas that are visible

Step 4. Plan for Painting: You can use any color of choice to paint as long as it will make your design look attractive. To paint there is a need for you to have a tape and expertly know how to Mark a line through a pencil, ruler and long straight material such as play wood.

Step 5. Paint the Design: The process of painting may actually span through some days, but if you actually dedicate time with some level of endurance you can mark it happening in just one day. You can make your painting look simple and easy but masking your tape with your pencil lines in several locations of your designs. At the same time, make use of varieties of colors.

Close to the end of the painting, you must slow down and allow one color to dry up before taping the next part. This is because there is not enough space again and if you do not exercise patience, you will end up making a mistake. You know that 2-3 coats of paint are needed in each space. The outdoor painting is easy because the air flow will dry it up quickly.

Get happy with your art and display it openly. You must determine where to display it by drilling the barn close to your target stud and place your quilt with a board already installed as a ledger. This ledger forms a sit when attaching the bolts.Once you place your quilt, use two bolts on the head and at the base of the quilt barn. At this time, remove the sit, and step a little bit backward to cross check your artwork, and appreciate it.

How to Create a Framed Barn Quilt

A framed barn quilt is beautiful and colorful, just like other great quilts you already learn to design in this book. Still, it is one quilt you can design from home for someone who probably means the world to you. Here's is how to create the quilt.

Required Materials

- Drill

- Exterior-grade screws

- Measuring tape and straight edge

- Paint, paintbrushes and a roller

- Painter's tape

- Circular saw

- D-rings and picture hanging wire

- One 4" x 8" x 3/4" sheet of plywood

- Two 1" x 4" x 8" frame

- Two 1" x 3" x 8" mat

- wood putty

- Pattern template

- Wood stain

- Pneumatic staple gun and staples

Instructions

Follow these simple steps to design your own framed barn quilt.

Step 1: Cut Plywood to Size: The Art is customarily a square. To begin, use a 4" by 8" sheet of plywood. Reduce it to appropriate size to contain the available space.

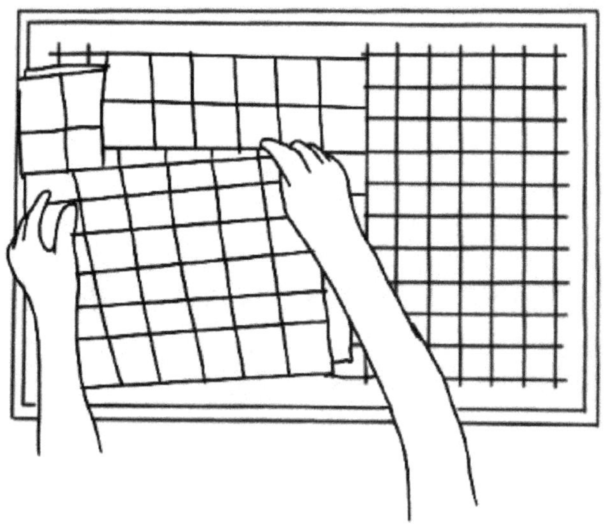

Step 2: Lay Out Design: Employ a vertical edge to mark out your project. Your design should have a square that is splitted into four triangles each. It is important to leave space of about two and half borders by the side of all your design to make it 1 by 3 wood matte. This will allow it to sit comfortably on the top of the canvas. You should try and slightly Mark each triangle with a colored pencil you intend to paint with to avoid mistakes.

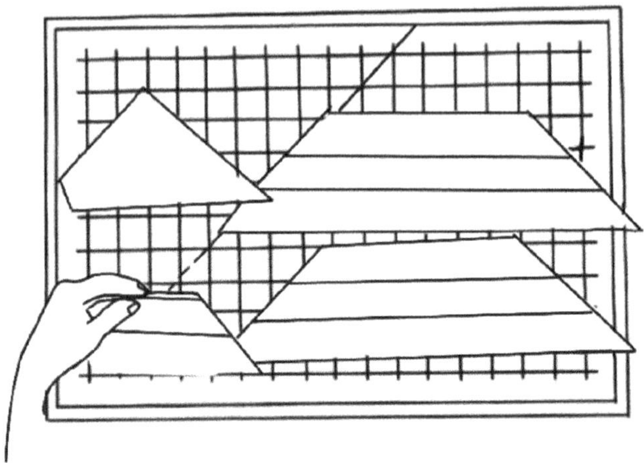

Step 4: Employ a tape to indicate all the sections for your slightest color. Make your paint start from the lightest color to deepest color. This will allow you to detect any mistake easily and mask it out. Put Paint on sections you have already taped-off. After this remove the tape from a 45-degree angle before the paint is dried up in order to have a clean side of the project.

Step 5: Tape and Paint Second Color: Now you are done with the first painting. Remove the tape from the lines in order to apply the next color. Maintain the same pattern used in the previous painting until you have successfully completed the painting of all sections.

Step 6: Add a Matte: A matte of 1" by 3" size should be cut to the angle of the canvas with 45-degree mitered corners. You should use a miter saw to cut this edge. Place them on the canvas to test if it will fit in. Join the four boards together with a staple gun. Use a wood glue at the back of the matte then let it lie on the top of the art. Add the matte to the canvas. Drill holes if you deem it fit.

Step 7: Frame It Up: The next step is to attach a 1 by 4 frame outside the matte. Make sure you join it with the edge of the canvass as well. Use a Miter saw to cut the four frame boards end to 42 meter long. Before you hammer all four pieces together, test them to know if they fit into the canvas.

Do another painting here in a desirous way. Join all four pieces together at the corners. Place your frame near the canvas and hammer it to the canvas and matte with screws from the outside edges.

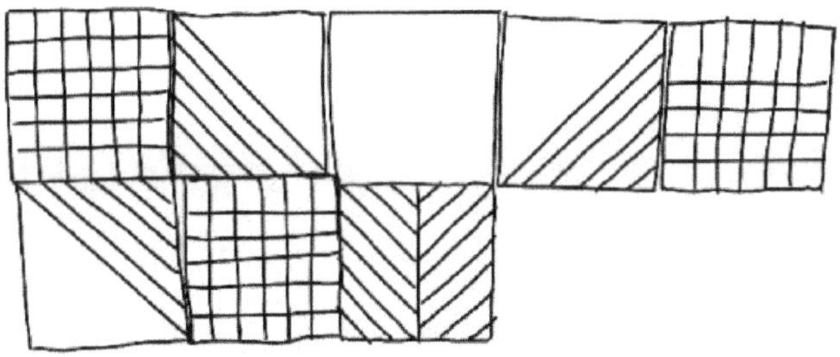

Step 8: Add Hanging Hardware: Add two rings with D patterns to the base of the board and securely insert a wrapping wire around the D-rings for a strong hold. Then hang your design for enjoyment.

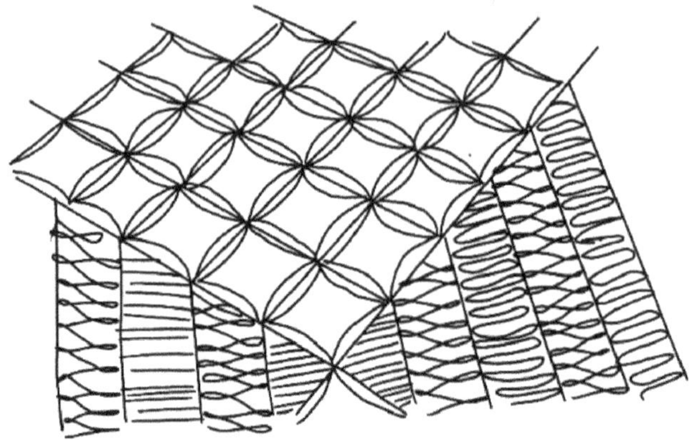

Chapter Summary

- Modern X quilts are bold, beautiful and charming but difficult to design.

- To create one, you need a bit of commitment and creativity.